Trish Stott

Highly Recommended **2**

Teacher's Book   Intermediate

English for the hotel and catering industry

OXFORD

UNIVERSITY PRESS

Introduction

Aims of the course

Highly Recommended 2 is designed to improve the job-related English of people who are training for, or who have already started, careers in the hotel and catering industry. The functional aspects of the course deal with the work routines of front office (receptionists, switchboard and reservations staff), restaurant (waiters/waitresses, kitchen and bar staff) and housekeeping (supervisors and room attendants). The course covers a variety of situations where employees have to use English with both customers and colleagues.

The course is intended for students starting at the pre-intermediate to intermediate level of language but suggestions are made throughout this Teacher's Book for adapting the material for classes of mixed ability. Also see the suggestions in the next section.

Structure of the course

The course consists of a Student's Book, Teacher's Book, Workbook and CD listening material. The Student's Book consists of twenty-eight units, most of which take the student through a number of hotel and restaurant situations and functions, beginning with phone enquiries and reservations through to payments and queries. Two units deal with situations a student travelling abroad might experience and explore the diversity of cultures and attitudes they might meet. The final three units deal with job skills, job applications and job interviews.

In addition to the functional focus, each unit presents new vocabulary and particular language points for study. Functions and structures are summarized in the Contents chart in the Student's Book, also reproduced here on pages 4–5. Although the units are arranged in a fairly logical sequence of topics, they need not be taught in this order as they are written as free-standing lessons. Teachers may choose to skip certain topics or may want a class to begin with the final three units if applying for jobs is the priority on starting the course.

Revision suggestions are given at the beginning of each unit of the Teacher's Book (after Unit 1) . At least 5–10 minutes' revision is recommended for each 90-minute lesson. Giving students adequate revision time is particularly important if the class is of mixed ability. The ratio of strong to weak students will determine where teachers choose to pitch the material. Here are

some suggestions for resolving classroom management and motivation difficulties with weaker students:

- encourage weaker and stronger students to work together
- allow more 'rehearsal time' before speaking activities
- allow weaker students to use their first language more frequently
- build in more writing stages before speaking activities
- allocate less demanding roles.

Here are some suggestions for stronger students:

- give a shorter time limit to complete exercises and activities
- insist on effective pronunciation and intonation during speaking activities
- challenge with extra vocabulary or different parts of speech
- have extra exercises ready for fast finishers
- give extended dictionary skills work
- allocate more demanding roles.

The communication objectives of the unit are listed under each unit title. Teachers and students can easily identify from these which job or jobs in the industry the unit is focusing on and whether it is of direct interest to them. Each unit is divided into the following sections:

Starter

This is intended as a warm-up to each unit. The activity often relates to a picture and gives weaker students a chance to participate by contributing information in their own language, which can then be translated into English and taught if appropriate. This section is an opportunity for the teacher to get the students' attention and enthusiasm by personalizing the material, and encouraging them to contribute from their own knowledge and experience.

The first Listening

In the majority of the units this is a dialogue or series of dialogues on the theme indicated by the unit title. Some of the Listening sections contain specialist vocabulary and so are quite demanding. It is important therefore to prepare students well before they listen. Pre-teach unfamiliar vocabulary and practise the pronunciation of items that students will have to recognize in order to complete the tasks. They will often need to listen to the recording more than once in order to complete a task. Answers to the tasks are given in the teaching notes at the relevant point. The first exercise in the section is a basic listening check. The second exercise is usually an intensive listening task, where students have to reproduce language from the recording. The third exercise is a controlled-practice speaking activity, which leads towards the more comprehensive Activity at the end of each unit. Teachers may like to work through the Expressions to learn, as well as recapping the language in exercise 2, before doing this third exercise.

Language study

Expressions to learn is a list of useful expressions from the first Listening. As a result, you may wish to ask students to cover this box while they are doing the listening exercises.

New words to use is an alphabetical list of the new words in the unit. These words are all in the Glossary at the back of the Student's Book. Teaching new vocabulary is an important part of every unit and is best done before the first Listening (note that there are some words from the second Listening in the New words to use list). Tips for teaching vocabulary:

- try to elicit the words by giving the context in the unit (use the pictures in the units)
- give definitions for students to guess
- give clues or descriptions relating to the words
- give synonyms, antonyms or symbols on the board
- give a different part of speech which may be more familiar
- ask stronger students to explain or translate
- have pronunciation and intonation practice to reinforce learning.

Language check introduces and practises points of grammar or a significant language area already met in the first Listening section. There are useful supplementary notes and exercises in the **Language review** section at the back of the Student's Book. These can be done as written work in class or given as homework but answers should be read aloud by students around the class. In addition there is a list of **Irregular verbs** on page 111 of the Student's Book.

The second Listening

This expands the theme of the unit and provides further listening practice. In most units a pair work activity is included in this section.

Activity

This consists of improvisations, role-plays and information gap activities based on the vocabulary and structures contained in the unit. The activities are designed to provide fluency practice, so students should not write the dialogues first. Most activities can be set up in a similar way:

- ask students to form pairs and tell them to look at the relevant information – try and make sure they do not look at each other's information
- model important and useful phrases and ask students to repeat them
- check pronunciation and intonation.

While students are doing the Activity, go around the class, checking and giving help where necessary. Make a note of mistakes, particularly in language already learnt, and write these on the whiteboard for students to correct. Finally, you could ask pairs of students to perform in front of the class. Time permitting, students could change partners and repeat the activity.

More words to use

This section can be found on pages 100–101 of the Student's Book. It contains extra vocabulary in word categories. The categories extend word groups already learnt in the unit. They stimulate and encourage students to expand their vocabulary in related topic areas. These words also appear in the Glossary.

Workbook

The Workbook exercises consolidate the work of the unit and are suitable as homework tasks. Each Workbook unit has a final exercise which practises the new words from More words to use.

Contents

UNIT	COMMUNICATIVE AREA	SITUATIONS/FUNCTIONS	STRUCTURES
15	Complaints and apologies	Acknowledging and apologizing Promising action	Present Perfect with *already*, *yet*, *just* *for* and *since*
16	Mistakes and problems	Checking details Finding a solution Offering compensation	Indirect questions: *Could you tell me …?* *Can you explain …? Do you know …?* etc.
17	Giving advice and assistance	Helping with lost luggage and lost passports Emergencies and first aid	First and second conditionals *unless*
18	Telephone communication problems	Difficult phone calls Clarifying, checking, repeating and spelling	The Passive
19	Conference and meeting enquiries	Talking about facilities and services Explaining conference packages	Managing a conversation: *Well, Now, So,* *Actually*
20	Handling payments	Dealing with guests' bills Payment security	Revision of numbers
21	Explaining and training	Kitchen hygiene and safety Following instructions Cooking processes	Obligation: *must, have to* No obligation: *don't have to, needn't* Prohibition: *mustn't, can't*
22	Working in housekeeping	Servicing a room The evening turndown service	*have something done: We had the* *windows cleaned last week.*
23	Health, safety and security	Health, safety and emergency procedures Security issues	*should/shouldn't* *ought to*
24	Countries and cultures	Making plans Talking about different customs	Verb + *-ing* Verb + (*to*) infinitive
25	Exploring different cultures	Differences between cultures Advising on cultural norms	Reporting verbs: *ask, warn, offer, advise,* *refuse, apologize for, assure, blame*
26	Working life	Talking about job skills and routines A celebrity chef's career moves	Adjective + preposition: *good at, kind to,* *interested in, pleased with*, etc.
27	Job applications	Personal qualities, skills and experience CVs and covering letters	Talking about the future: *going to* and *will* Question tags
28	Job interviews	Interview questions and answers Interview tips	Past Simple or Present Perfect?

1 Dealing with incoming calls

↬ **Situations/functions**
Receiving incoming phone calls
Taking messages
Dealing with requests
↬ **Structures**
Offers: *Can/Could*, *Would you like to*, *I'll*
Requests: *I'd like to*, *Can/Could*

■ Starter

Elicit the meaning of *front office* and *switchboard*. Front office includes reception or front desk plus the switchboard and other staff who deal directly with customers. Check if any students work or have worked on a switchboard. Ask for examples of the kinds of calls a hotel switchboard often deals with. Read situations 1–5 and ask students to match them with the pictures a–e.

Answers

1 c	2 a	3 e	4 b	5 d

■ Listening *Working in front office*

Pre-teach unfamiliar vocabulary from New words to use (see Introduction for suggestions). Note that there are some words from the second Listening in the list. Try to elicit the meaning of the words by giving the context: *You … the phone when it rings. / You … later when someone's not at home. / You ask someone to … while you transfer their call.* Practise pronunciation of more difficult words so that students can identify them in the Listening: *answer, put through.*

1 ⌕ **1.1** Tell students to read the sentences. Play the recording and ask them to underline the correct alternative. Play the calls again, one by one, and check answers.

Answers

1 book a room	5	256
2 he's not in his office	6	the line's busy
3 Mr Cole is late	7	says he'll call back
4 table	8	the phone is ringing

2 ⌕ **1.1** Ask students to read sentences 1–8. Stronger students may be able to fill in the gaps without listening again. Play the recording and ask students to complete the sentences. Check answers around the class. Has

everybody got the short forms in numbers 3, 6, and 8? Stress that in spoken English, short forms are good, natural English. Ask students to read the sentences aloud and check pronunciation and intonation.

Answers

1 speaking, I help you	5	book a table
2 put you through	6	line's busy
3 's calling	7	to leave
4 I take	8	'll call back

Practise the Expressions to learn before doing exercise 3.

3 The flow diagrams are prompts for making four calls between hotel switchboard and callers. Ask students to form pairs and sit back to back. Remind them to use the sentences they completed in exercise 2 and the expressions. Ask them to work through each call and then change roles and repeat the calls. Go around the class, checking accuracy and polite intonation. Make a note of any problem areas and model the sentence or phrase for them. Get students to repeat individually and chorally. Suggest that some students perform their dialogues in front of the class.

■ Language study

Expressions to learn

Ask students to read the expressions aloud. Check pronunciation and intonation. Ask them to learn the expressions for homework.

New words to use

Ask students to check any words that are still unfamiliar in the Glossary. Elicit the words from around the class by giving students prompts: a sentence to finish, an opposite or synonym, a clue to the word, a definition of its meaning. Ask students to learn the new words for homework.

Language check

Can/Could, Would you like to, I'll

How much time you spend on this depends on the level of your students. If strong students find the Language check easy, move on after a quick revision. Write the target structures for offering help on the board. Point out that the first two are in the form of questions. *Can* is more natural than *Could* in offers of help.

1 Ask students to complete the exercise using the target structures. Check answers around the class.

Answers

1 Would you like to	5 Would you like to
2 I'll	6 Can/Could
3 Can/Could	7 I'll
4 I'll	8 Would you like to

I'd like to, Can/Could

Write the target structures for making requests on the board. *Can* and *Could* are very similar. *Could* is considered slightly more polite. Point out that we often add *please* at the end of requests.

2 Ask students to look at the lists of incoming calls (1–6) and switchboard responses (a–f) and to match them. Check answers around the class.

Answers

1 e 2 a 3 f 4 c 5 b 6 d	

Ask students to read the example dialogue. Then ask them to work with a partner to make requests and offer help using the prompts. Go around the class, checking that students are using *I'd like to* for the requests. *Can/Could* is not incorrect just less used in this context. Encourage the use of *please* at the end of requests. All the responses begin with *I'll* except f (*Can/Could I have your …?*).

■ Listening *Customer requests*

Elicit the topics in the Listening by asking questions such as: *Why do guests call reception to advise of late arrival?* (to hold the rooms) / *When guests have a child with them what do they request?* (extra bed) / *What does the receptionist need in order to book a parking space?* (car registration).

1 🎧 **1.2** Ask students to read the sentences. Play the recording and ask students to mark them *true* or *false*. Play the recording again with pauses for students to check their answers.

Answers

1 false	3 true	5 true	7 false
2 true	4 false	6 false	

2 🎧 **1.2** Ask students to read the sentences. Play the recording again and ask students to number the sentences in the order they're said in the dialogue.

Answers

a 7 b 3 c 1 d 6 e 4 f 8 g 2 h 5	

Point out the usage: *What name is it?* (not *What name are you?*); *That's fine.* (*That* = what was requested – to hold the room); the useful phrase *anything else*, meaning 'anything more'.

If there's time, you could ask students to practise the sentences in pairs. Check polite intonation.

3 Remind students of the target structures *Can/Could* and *I'd like to/I'll*. Ask them to work in pairs to write or make notes for a dialogue using the prompts. Write the first line on the board: *Good morning, Hotel … . How can I help you?* Go around the class, helping weaker students. When they are ready, students can practise their dialogues.

■ Activity

Tell students they are going to practise dealing with incoming calls. With weaker students, you may like to do a quick revision of the target structures and any words or phrases they have had difficulty with. Divide the class into pairs, Student A and Student B, and ask them to sit back to back. Direct them to their roles. Ask them to read their own role, but not to look at their partner's. It is important for this stage of the unit to have an information gap so that free practice of the calls can occur. When they have read the information, ask Student A to start the first call: *Good afternoon, Palace Hotel. … speaking. Can I help you?* Tell students to use their own names for the greeting. Go around the class, helping students where necessary. Ask students to note down the requests made when they are in the role of receptionist. When all the calls are finished, students can turn round and check the accuracy of the information they noted. Go over general problems with the class, particularly any expressions you heard which were impolite or inappropriate.

■ More words to use

Write these words on the board: *beep, dial tone, directory, hang up, local call, long distance call, operator, outside line.* Tell students to look up any new words in the Glossary. Ask students to read the words aloud and check pronunciation.

2 Customer information

⟶ **Situations/functions**
Giving information to customers
Answering questions about hotel facilities and services

⟶ **Structures**
Is there?/Are there?, *There's/There are*, *There isn't/There aren't*
Prepositions of location

■ Revision of Unit 1

Expressions to learn

Elicit expressions for dealing with incoming calls by giving prompts: *Someone wants to book a room. / Transfer the call to reservations. / The line is busy.* With a weaker group, ask them to read the list of expressions and then give prompts in a different order to the list.

New words to use / More words to use

Make flashcards of the words. Give students one word each, which they do not show to anyone. Depending on the level of your class, ask them to: explain the meaning of the word in English; give a sentence with the word in context; translate the word into their native language.

Other revision suggestions

- Get students to practise dialogues in pairs, reading the Listening script from Unit 1.
- Tell students to do the Activity from Unit 1, working with a different partner.

■ Starter

Tell students to look at the pictures. Explain that they show the facilities and services in Hotel-Royal, an international 5-star hotel. Help students to explain what the facilities and services are (e.g. *Wi-Fi* – wireless Internet access) and write them on the board. Find out if any students have worked in a hotel and ask them to describe the facilities and services there. Continue the list already on the board. Encourage students to add any more facilities/services they know.

■ Listening *Giving information*

Pre-teach unfamiliar vocabulary from New words to use (see Introduction). Note that there are some words from the second Listening in the list. Practise pronunciation of any difficult words so that students can identify them in the Listening.

1 🎧 2.1 Tell students to read the list of facilities and services. Play the recording and ask them to tick the items they hear. Check answers around the class.

Answers

1, 4, 6, 7

2 🎧 2.1 Ask students to read sentences 1–8. Stronger students will be able to predict the missing words. Play the recording and ask students to complete the sentences. Check answers around the class. Ask students to read the sentences aloud and check pronunciation and intonation.

Answers

1 do you get	5 What about, Is there
2 from, to	6 on the
3 leave from	7 hire
4 how long	8 come to, car rental

Practise the Expressions to learn before doing exercise 3.

3 Ask students to look at the hotel information. Write *Is there?*, *Can you/I?*, *I'd like to*, *Where?*, *How long?* on the board as prompts for questions. Ask students to work in pairs to do the activity (the student asking questions should cover the information). Encourage them to ask more than one question about each thing. Go around the class, checking accuracy and polite intonation. Suggest that some students perform their dialogues in front of the class. With stronger students, you could relate this activity to their local area or create an information gap by using hotels and airports that only some students know.

■ Language study

Expressions to learn

Ask students to read the expressions aloud. Check pronunciation and intonation. Ask students to complete the unfinished sentences with phrases of their own. Ask them to learn the expressions for homework.

New words to use

Elicit the words from around the class by giving students prompts: a sentence to finish, an opposite or synonym, a clue to the word, a definition of its meaning. Ask students to check any words that are still unfamiliar in the Glossary. Ask students to learn the new words for homework.

Language check

Is there?/Are there?, There's/There are, There isn't/There aren't

How much time you spend on this depends on the level of your students. If strong students find it easy, move on after a quick revision. Write the different forms on the board. Point out the pronunciation and use of the short form *there's* in spoken English. Remind them not to use it for short answers, e.g. *Yes, there is.*

1 Ask students to read the example and to look at the pictures again. Then ask them to work in pairs to ask and answer about 1–10. Go around the class, helping, correcting and making suggestions. Correct and model any errors.

Prepositions of location

Tell students to study the diagrams. Check if the meanings are clear. Model any meanings that aren't clear with items in the classroom.

2 Ask students to look at the pictures. Complete the sentences by asking students around the class. Check each answer with the rest of the class and discuss and clarify any that are not correct.

Answers

1 next to the currency exchange
2 at the top of the stairs
3 behind the reception desk
4 between the business centre and the lifts
5 inside the lift
6 above the restaurant

■ Listening *Services and facilities*

1 🎧 2.2 Tell students they are going to hear a short presentation about the Sofia, a 5-star hotel. Ask them to look at the list of services and facilities, and fill in any missing words they can predict. Play the recording and ask them to complete the list. Play the recording again with pauses and correct the exercise around the class, making sure that everyone contributes. Model any pronunciation difficulties and get students to repeat after you.

Answers

1 centre	6 shuttle service	11 high-speed
2 indoor shopping	7 parking	12 pay-per-view
3 main tourist	8 currency	13 separate
4 24-hour	9 tour	14 exercise
5 checkout	10 access	

2 Ask students to look at the four categories and give one or two examples of each, preferably not those from the Listening. Ask students to work in pairs or four small groups to match all the items in exercise 1 to the categories. Only give them a few minutes, depending on ability. Ask for answers around the class or for each group to contribute a category.

Answers

1 24-hour front desk, express checkout, airport shuttle service, currency exchange, car rental desk, tour desk
2 air conditioning, high-speed Internet access, pay-per-view movies, separate tub and shower
3 near city centre, near indoor shopping mall, near main tourist attractions
4 free parking, business centre, lifts, wheelchair access, exercise gym and sauna

3 If the class has Internet access, ask them to research different hotels around the world for more 5-star services and facilities.

■ Activity

Tell students they are going to prepare a short presentation using the four headings – similar to the one about the Sofia. They can use the information on page 60, think of a hotel they already know or research a hotel on the Internet. Depending on classroom facilities, students could prepare a short PowerPoint presentation for homework. Only allow notes for when presentations are given as this is fluency practice. Be positive about *all* presentations before suggesting improvements. If you have a large group, presentation work may not be practicable. You could play a 'One-upmanship' game. Pre-teach phrases such as *Uh, really, That's nothing, Well, listen to this.* Students brainstorm their hotel information in small groups and offer one piece of information to the class, e.g. *Our hotel has got a private beach.* Another group joins in with *That's nothing! Our hotel has got a private beach and three swimming pools*, and so on.

More words to use

Write these words on the board: *babysitting, cot* (US *crib*), *dry cleaning, lift* (US *elevator*), *hair dryer, iron, jacuzzi, laundry, luggage storage, room service, safe deposit box, wake-up service.* Tell students to look up any new words in the Glossary. Ask students to read the words aloud and check pronunciation.

3 Taking reservations

Situations/functions
Taking room reservations
Confirming details of a booking
Changing and cancelling reservations

Structures
Prepositions of time

■ Revision of Unit 2

Expressions to learn

Ask for examples of hotel services and facilities. Elicit expressions by asking questions and giving prompts: *How do hotel guests often get from the airport to the hotel? / Recommend a good French restaurant.* Also ask questions to elicit prepositions of location: *Where is the business centre / breakfast buffet?* With a weaker group, ask them to read the list of expressions and then give prompts in a different order.

New words to use / More words to use

Make flashcards of the words plus names of other facilities and services that came up in the unit. The varied vocabulary in Unit 2 gives a good opportunity for group or team activities miming, translating or giving a definition of the words. Mark your flash cards *M, T* or *D* as you think best. Divide the class into two performing and two guessing groups, A and B. Give the 'performers' (who will be on one side of the room) their flashcards. Students take turns to present their flashcards to the guessing team, who score points for guessing the correct word. Change roles half way through the words.

Other revision suggestions

- Get students to practise dialogues in pairs, reading the first Listening script from Unit 2.
- Tell students to do the Activity from Unit 2, working with a different partner.

■ Starter

Dealing with room reservations is one of the most important jobs in a hotel. The most widely-used hotel reservation software is Fidelio. Ask if students in work are familiar with it or what alternative they have used. How do they take reservations? What questions do they ask the guest? Alternatively, ask students without experience what they think happens. Pre-teach any relevant vocabulary from New words to use. Elicit the words using questions, prompts and a sample

credit card. Ask students to work in pairs to make a list of all the information the receptionist needs when taking a room booking.

■ Listening *Taking a room reservation*

Elicit the problems related to phone bookings, e.g. taking names and dates accurately (difficulties with telephoning are dealt with in Unit 18). Ask for ways of dealing with problems, e.g. spell names and repeat information. Pre-teach remaining unfamiliar vocabulary from New words to use (see Introduction and Unit 1 for suggestions). Practise pronunciation of any difficult words so that students can identify them in the Listening: *expiry date, type.* Also point out syllable stress as in CONtact number, deDUCT.

1 🎧 **3.1** Ask students to look at their list of required information from the Starter and to amend or add to it as they listen to the recording. Ask them to compare their lists in pairs before you give the answers.

Answers

> surname, country of caller, arrival and departure day and date, number of nights, number of adults, number of children, number of rooms, type of room, contact name, contact number, credit card details to secure reservation

2 🎧 **3.1** Ask students to read sentences 1–8. Stronger students will already be able to fill in the gaps. Play the recording and ask students to complete the sentences. Play again and check their answers. Point out the difference between written and spoken dates: *10 May* or *10th May* is said *the tenth of May.* Ask students to read the sentences aloud and check pronunciation and intonation.

Answers

1 book accommodation, group	5 rate, the single
2 'll arrive, the, of	6 probably, late in, at
3 need, two single	7 give me, on the back
4 just check	8 look forward, seeing, on

Practise the Expressions to learn before doing exercise 3. Then turn to the telephone alphabet on page 101 of the Student's Book. Select a number of students, with difficult names if possible, to take turns saying their names. The other students ask: *Could you spell that, please?* The students then spell their names using the telephone alphabet.

3   Ask students to work in pairs to do the activity, thinking of their own guest information for the items listed. Give help with information for lower-level groups. Go around the class, checking accuracy and polite intonation. Make sure that students change roles. Make a note of any problem areas and model the sentence or phrase for them. Suggest that some students perform their dialogues in front of the class.

■ Language study

Expressions to learn

Ask students to read the expressions aloud. Check pronunciation and intonation. Ask them to learn the expressions for homework.

New words to use

Elicit the words from around the class by giving students prompts (see Introduction for suggestions). Ask students to learn the new words for homework.

Language check

Prepositions of time

Look at the list of prepositions together. Ask students to explain the difference between *a.m.* (before noon) and *p.m.* (after noon). Note that 12 noon is 12 p.m. Also elicit the difference between *by midnight* (before) and *at midnight* (precisely 12 a.m.). Point out the irregularity: *in the morning/afternoon/evening* but *at night*. Ask students to complete the exercise. Check answers orally around the class.

Answers

1 for, from, to	3 by	5 for, during
2 on, at	4 at, until	6 at, after

■ Listening *Changing and cancelling reservations*

1   Check that students understand the meaning of changing and cancelling reservations. Ask them to look at the four Fidelio reservation screens then read sentences 1–8 and mark them *true* or *false*. Go around the class, checking answers. Elicit the correct information for the false sentences.

Answers

1 true	3 false	5 false	7 false
2 true	4 true	6 false	8 true

2   🎧 3.2 Play the recording and ask students to make a note of the changes to the four reservation screens in their notebooks. Tell them to compare notes with a partner. Play the recording again, call by call, for students to check their answers.

Answers

Feinds	Nights: 6; Departure: 16 May Friday; Adults: 7; Room Type: 2 double, 3 single
Marsh	cancelled
Olson	Adults: 2; Room Type: double; Contact number: 0046 7896 1744 09
Wong	Surname: Lee

3   Ask students to work in pairs as caller and receptionist to practise changing reservations. Ask them to choose one of the reservation screens. They should decide on two changes they want to make and then call the hotel. The student playing the receptionist should answer the call and make a note of any changes. Then students change roles and choose a different screen and changes.

■ Activity

Tell students they are going to practise changing reservations. Divide the class into pairs, Student A and Student B. Ask them to sit back to back. Direct them to their roles. Ask them to read their own role, but not to look at their partner's. When students have read the information, ask Student B to start the first call: *Good afternoon, Pacific Hotel. How can I help you?* Ask Student B to complete the screen on page 63 with the reservation details. Then Student A calls again to change the reservation. Student B should note the changes. When the two calls are finished, the students can turn round and check the accuracy of the information they noted. With lower-level students, you may prefer to handle the calls in two stages: after call 1, check the information; after call 2, check the changes. Then Student A begins the next two calls: *Good afternoon, George Hotel. How can I help you?* When all calls are finished, go over general problems with the class, particularly any expressions you heard which were impolite or inappropriate.

■ More words to use

Write these words on the board: *reservation, information, cancellation, location*. Tell students to look up the words in a dictionary and to find the corresponding verb. Ask students to read the words aloud and check pronunciation.

4 Dealing with booking enquiries

→ **Situations/functions**
Turning down bookings
Giving explanations
Suggesting alternatives

→ **Structures**
Present Simple and Present Continuous
Short forms

■ Revision of Unit 3

Expressions to learn

Elicit expressions by asking questions and giving prompts: *Ask for a customer's name. / Ask to spell name. / Spell your own name. / Ask for a contact number. / Why ask for credit card details on booking? / What credit card details are needed?*

New words to use / More words to use

Make flashcards of the words (see Unit 2).

Other revision suggestions

- Ask students questions about their timetables/ routines to elicit prepositions of time. Write prepositions on the board, e.g. *during, until, before, after, by,* and indicate that you want an answer to include a certain preposition.
- Get students to practise dialogues in pairs, reading the Listening scripts from Unit 3.
- Tell students to do the Activity from Unit 3, working with a different partner.

■ Starter

Tell students to look at the pictures. Ask what hotels have to do if they get an enquiry and the hotel is full (they have to *turn down* the booking). Tell students not to get confused with *turndown service,* which is dealt with in Unit 22. This is the housekeeping service of preparing a guest bedroom for the night. Ask what other reasons a hotel/restaurant may have for turning down bookings (booked for a function, refurbishment, closed for a holiday, emergency repairs). Encourage students to talk about their own work experiences.

■ Listening *Dealing with booking enquiries*

Pre-teach unfamiliar vocabulary from New words to use (see Introduction). Always ask stronger students if they can explain or translate the words. Model sentences with *(be) left* and *(have) left* meaning 'remaining':

There are three doubles and two twins left for tonight. Have you got any family rooms left for those dates? Also model sentences for *instead* meaning 'as an alternative': *I can offer you a twin instead of a double.* Practise pronunciation of any difficult words so that students can identify them in the Listening.

1 🎧 **4.1** Tell students they are going to hear five booking enquiries. Ask them to look at the example for call 1. Play the recording and ask students to complete the table. Ask them to compare their tables in pairs before you give the answers.

Answers

> 2 a double room for two nights
>   There're no double rooms left.
> 3 a family room for one week
>   The hotel's closed.
> 4 a table for ten for lunch
>   The restaurant's busy.
> 5 a table with view of the harbour
>   The tables with a view are all reserved.

2 🎧 **4.1** Ask students to put the phrases in the correct order to make sentences from the Listening. Play the recording again and check answers around the class. Ask students to read the sentences aloud and check pronunciation and intonation.

Answers

> 1 One moment, please.
> 2 We're fully booked that night.
> 3 I'd like to book a double room for two nights.
> 4 I'm afraid we don't have any double rooms left for those dates.
> 5 Unfortunately, the hotel's closed that week for refurbishment.
> 6 We're not reopening till Saturday the 9th of March.
> 7 I'm sorry, but we're very busy that day with a business conference.
> 8 How many is it for?

Practise the Expressions to learn before doing exercise 3.

3 Ask students to form pairs and sit back to back. Ask them to read the prompts and check everyone understands what to do. Make sure they take turns to be caller and receptionist. Fast finishers could replay the roles, changing the reason for turning down the booking. Go around the class, checking accuracy and polite intonation. Make a note of any problem areas and model the sentence or phrase for them. Suggest

that some students perform their dialogues in front of the class. You could ask students to write their conversations, as a classroom follow-up or homework activity.

■ Language study

Expressions to learn

Ask students to read the expressions aloud. Draw their attention to the short forms used. Check pronunciation and intonation. Ask students to complete the unfinished sentences with phrases of their own. Ask them to learn the expressions for homework.

New words to use

Elicit the words from around the class by giving students prompts (see Unit 1). Ask students to learn the new words for homework.

Language check
Present Simple

Ask students to read the examples. Explain that the first sentence refers to a fact or piece of information and the second is a repeated action, routine or habit. Give and ask for further examples.

Present Continuous

Look at the examples and ask how the tense is used. Confirm the use for talking about things happening now and for future arrangements. Give and ask for further examples.

Short forms

Remind students about the use of short forms (or contractions) in spoken and informal written English. Refer them back to the Expressions to learn for further examples. Ask students to complete the exercise. Check the answers orally around the class.

Answers

1 enjoy	6 's
2 'm, 're closing	7 'm travelling, 'm staying
3 has	8 looks, prefer
4 Do you take	9 don't know, 's preparing
5 isn't, 's showing	10 Are you eating

■ Listening *Suggesting an alternative*

1   Discuss how suggesting an alternative when bookings are turned down is good for customer service/customer relations and possibly good for sales – therefore good for business. Ask students to work in small groups and list alternatives from their own working or life experience. Ask them to turn back to the first Listening exercise and suggest alternatives that could be offered to those callers.

2   🎧 4.2 Tell students they are going to listen to reception suggesting alternatives to the callers in 🎧 4.1. Ask them to underline the correct alternatives. Ask them to compare their answers with the list they made before listening. Go over the answers with the class.

Answers

1 trying the Station Hotel
2 a family room
3 calling a hotel in a different town
4 a table in the Terrace Bar
5 a table at the window with a different view

3   🎧 4.2 Play the recording again and ask students to mark whether the callers accept the alternatives.

Answers

1 yes   2 yes   3 no   4 no   5 yes

4   Ask students to work in pairs, as caller and receptionist or restaurant staff, to practise suggesting and responding to alternatives. They can use the alternatives in exercise 2 or think of their own.

■ Activity

Tell students they are going make and receive two calls each, practising the language from the unit. Divide the class into pairs, Student A and Student B. Ask them to sit back to back. Direct them to their roles. Ask them to read their own role, but not to look at their partner's. Ask Student B to start the first call: *Hello, Pines Hotel. How can I help you?* Go around the class, helping students where necessary. Go over general problems with the class, particularly any expressions you heard which were impolite or inappropriate. Students can then do the activity again, using the empty charts on page 64 to make a note of their own information. Stronger groups could go straight to this part of the activity.

■ More words to use

See Workbook page 11 for an exercise which extends on some of the new words from the unit.

5 Correspondence

⇢ **Situations/functions**
Writing letters and emails to customers
Responding to emails and voicemails

⇢ **Structures**
Greetings and endings in correspondence

■ Revision of Unit 4

Expressions to learn

Elicit expressions by asking questions and giving prompts. What would students say if: *hotel was fully booked that night / no rooms left for the dates / hotel closed for refurbishment / restaurant is full with a business conference / all tables with a view reserved*? Check that students are using short forms when speaking.

New words to use

Make flashcards of the words (see Unit 2).

Other revision suggestions

• Write example sentences for the use of the Present Simple and Present Continuous on the board and ask students to explain them. Ask students to give their own sentences using the tenses. Give prompts if necessary: *What's the name of your street? / What do you usually do on Sundays? / What are you doing now? / What's happening at the weekend?*
• Get students to practise dialogues in pairs, reading the Listening script from Unit 4.
• Tell students to do the Activity from Unit 4, working with a different partner.

■ Starter

Discuss the importance of accurate written communication. A reply to an email may be a customer's first contact with a hotel, so it's important to create a good impression. Talk about the decline of letter writing with the increasing use of emails and texting. Stress though, that although emails between friends or colleagues may be brief and informal, emails to customers often have to give a lot of information and must be courteous and written in good, clear language. Ask working students about work emails they write. Find out if they have any difficulties or concerns about writing them. Make a list on the board of different reasons a hotel may email or write to a customer:

confirmation of a reservation, change or cancellation, suggestion of alternative dates or hotel, apology for delay or error, information about transfer, directions, information about facilities and services. Advise students that using model emails or letters is a good way to start off writing to customers. Sometimes only names, dates and room types have to be changed. Some hotels may have standard models available for staff to use.

■ Writing *Letters and emails*

Ask students to look at the three pieces of correspondence in pairs. Elicit what the topics are (1 information/directions 2 confirmation of bookings 3 change of dates not possible).

1–3 Look at the phrases together and ask students to complete the relevant gaps in each email/letter.

Answers

1	1 a	2 b	3 c		
2	1 b	2 c	3 a		
3	1 a	2 b	3 c		

Check for any problems with vocabulary or understanding. Ask students to read the completed correspondence aloud. Stress that written communication should always be read through before sending as simple mistakes, even by native speakers, can often be made. Ask students about any differences between the emails and the letter – really it's only the layout. The ending (*Yours sincerely*) and possibly the third gap in the letter (*We hope we may be of*) are a bit formal for an email, but it wouldn't be a mistake to use them. You could ask students to write/key in the completed correspondence and to keep them as models.

4 Ask students about the language they use in emails. Probably they will tell you about the informality and abbreviations they use. Pre-teach unfamiliar vocabulary from New words to use (see Introduction). Read through the tips for business emails and discuss them. Ask questions like: *Why is it important to complete the subject line?* (useful for receiver) / *What greetings/endings do you know? / Why have different paragraphs? / Why not use abbreviations to customers?* (may not understand) / *Why not use capital letters to stress something?* (looks impolite and is considered the equivalent of shouting)

Ask someone to read the email to Carlos Lomo aloud. Ask for comments and write them on the board: *tone is too informal, layout wrong, abbreviations used, ending too informal.* Ask students to rewrite the email in pairs. Get students to read their answers aloud and ask for suggestions for improvement. Always comment constructively before suggesting correction. See page 62 for a photocopiable model answer.

Language study

Expressions to learn

Ask students to read the expressions. Check understanding. Ask students to learn the expressions for homework.

New words to use

Elicit the words from around the class by giving students prompts (see Unit 2). Ask students to learn the new words for homework.

Language check

Overview of greetings and endings

This may already be familiar to students. Point out the difference in formality between language for people you know very well and for customers.

1 Do the exercise around the class and compare answers with the models given in the key.

Model answers

> 1 Dear Mr Dupont, Best regards
> 2 Dear Aldo and Maria, Best wishes
> 3 Hi Tom, All the best
> 4 Dear Ms Beale, Regards
> 5 Dear Sir or Madam, Yours faithfully

2 Ask students to rewrite the letter in a more formal business style. Check sentences in the letter orally around the class. See page 62 for a photocopiable model answer.

Listening *Customer messages*

Large hotels will have a 24-hour switchboard, but restaurants/smaller hotels may have a voicemail service. Elicit what sorts of messages customers might leave.

1 🎧 5.1 Tell students they are going to hear five voicemail messages from customers. Ask them to note down a summary of what each caller wants. Play the recording. Check answers around the class. Discuss and correct any misunderstandings.

Answers

> 1 to reserve an ensuite, twin room for three nights from 6 to 9 January
> 2 to change a booking to three doubles and three singles for seven nights from 10 May
> 3 to check her booking dates and email her
> 4 to book a table for ten on 13 July at 1 p.m.
> 5 information about special events (wedding party on 25 June next year)

2 🎧 5.1 Depending on the level of your students, you can ask them to reply to all five voicemails or just choose two. First ask them to look at their notes for each message and the prompts for the reply. Give them only two or three minutes to write each reply. Explain that this is to get them used to the idea of quick correspondence in a work situation.

3 Ask students to check their replies with a partner. Ask some students to read their replies aloud. See page 62 for photocopiable model answers.

Activity

Tell students they are going to write an email and a letter, practising the language from the unit.

1 Ask students to read the email tips again and the information in the Language check. Tell them to read the instructions for the email and check they understand. Give them ten minutes to write and read through their email response. Ask them to compare their email with a partner and see if any improvements can be made. Ask some students to read their email (or a sentence from the email) aloud. Correct mistakes and inappropriate language, and model alternatives.

2 Remind students about the layout of a letter: address and date; short clear sentences; new paragraphs for new topics. Read the instructions for the letter together and check that everything is clear. Give students 15 minutes to write and read through their letter. Ask them to compare their letter with a partner and see if any improvements can be made. Ask some students to read their letter aloud. Correct mistakes and inappropriate language, and model appropriate alternatives. See page 62 for photocopiable model answers.

More words to use

Write these abbreviations on the board: *asap, encs, incl, no, plc, pp, re, rd, st, cc.* Tell students to look them up in a dictionary.

6 Welcoming guests

Situations/functions
Making guests feel welcome
Checking guests into their accommodation
Giving essential information

Structures
Possessive adjectives
Object pronouns

■ Revision of Unit 5

Expressions to learn

Elicit expressions by asking questions about sentences used in correspondence: *confirmation of room or table reservation / first line of request to change dates or number or type of rooms / enclosed information / final polite sentence for reply to information request / reply saying hotel is fully booked / reply offering accommodation at a partner hotel.*

New words to use

Make flashcards of the words (see Unit 2).

Other revision suggestions

- Give examples of letter or email beginnings or endings and elicit the corresponding phrase, e.g. letter – *Dear Sir* (*Yours faithfully*). You could ask students to write on the board or spell the answers.
- Tell students to write either the letter or email from the Activity in Unit 5, working with a different partner.

■ Starter

Ask students with work experience about check-in procedures in their hotels. Elicit what information is needed at check-in and make a list on the board. Go over unfamiliar vocabulary and model pronunciation. Ask for ideas on handling group arrivals efficiently with good customer service. Brainstorm situations that guests dislike at check-in. Then ask students to look at the pictures. Elicit what they can see and discuss how hotels can make check-in a positive experience. Ask students with work experience for anecdotes about guests in check-in situations.

■ Listening *Dealing with arrivals*

Pre-teach remaining unfamiliar vocabulary from New words to use (see Introduction). Practise pronunciation of more difficult words so that students can identify them in the Listening: *details, patience, ready, sign, voucher.*

1 🎧 6.1 Tell students to read 1–9. Check understanding. Play the recording and ask students to tick the information that is on the printout. Check answers around the class. Play the recording again with pauses for students to check their answers. Check the list on the board from the Starter and get students to add any missing items to the list.

Answers

2, 4, 7, 8, 9

2 🎧 6.1 Ask students to read sentences 1–9 and try to predict the missing words in pairs. Play the recording again and ask students to check their answers. Ask them to read the sentences aloud and check pronunciation and intonation.

Answers

1 take, welcome	6 sign here
2 your name, check you in	7 here's
3 passports, vouchers	8 room number is, the
4 Thank you, your	second
5 registration details	9 take your luggage

3 Ask students to look at the flow chart showing the sequence of the check-in procedure. Ask them to read the Expressions to learn and get them to identify, in pairs, which expressions go with the various stages in the flow chart. Ask them to work with a partner, taking turns as receptionist and guest to practise dialogues dealing with arrivals. The guest role will be fairly minimal with active listening phrases like: *Thank you, Fine, Right, OK, Here you are.* Go around the class, checking accuracy and polite intonation. Make sure that students change roles. If there are any problem areas, refer students to the expressions. Suggest that some students perform their dialogues in front of the class.

■ Language study

Expressions to learn

Ask students to read the expressions aloud. Check pronunciation and intonation. Ask students to learn the expressions for homework.

New words to use

Elicit the words from around the class by giving students prompts. Ask students to learn the new words for homework.

Language check

Possessive adjectives

Elicit the possessive adjectives around the class by pointing at objects and people: *her book, my bag, their table*, etc. Write them on the board.

Object pronouns

Write a sentence on the board: *The receptionist spoke to the man (to him).* Elicit the parts of the sentence: verb (*spoke*), subject (*receptionist*), object (*man*), object pronoun (*him*). Elicit the remaining object pronouns with similar sentences and write them on the board. Study the sentences in the examples together. Note that *Collect* and *Enjoy* are imperative forms, so the subject is understood as *you* but not written.

1 Ask students to read sentences 1–8 and underline the correct alternative, either the possessive adjective or the object pronoun. Correct answers around the class, analysing any errors. Draw attention to *its* in number 7. There is no apostrophe even though it's a possessive. *It's* is always the short form for *it is.*

Answers

1 me, my	3 them	5 him	7 its
2 our	4 his	6 your	8 us

■ Listening *When and where?*

Look at the pictures again together. Ask questions to review vocabulary. Brainstorm questions the guests might ask the receptionist when they check in. Do a quick revision of telling the time by writing times on the board. Keep to the easy, well-known way: *seven thirty, eight twenty-three, one forty-five.* Remind students that we don't speak the 24-hour clock unless it's a travel departure or arrival timetable, e.g. *His flight leaves at twenty fifteen* (20.15). So, we say *seven thirty a.m.* or *seven thirty in the morning.* Check that students are familiar with the American phrase *24/7* (24 hours a day, seven days a week).

1 🎧 6.2 Ask students to tick the correct information as they listen to the recording. Play the recording again so they can check their answers. Check answers around the class. Correct and model any mistakes in pronunciation or intonation with students repeating after you.

Answers

1 the first floor restaurant	5 the Terrace Restaurant
2 7.30 to 10.00 a.m.	6 7.00 to 9.30 p.m.
3 24 hours	7 9.00 a.m.
4 on the top floor	8 in the hotel shop

2 Ask students to read the example dialogue. Ask them to work with a partner to make similar dialogues, using the information in the previous exercise. Go around the class, helping and correcting where necessary. Pay particular attention to polite intonation in the receptionist's answers. Correct and model common errors and get students to repeat after you individually and chorally.

■ Activity

Tell students they are going to practise checking in a guest. Divide the class into pairs, Student A and Student B, and direct them to their roles. Ask them to read their own role, but not to look at their partner's. It is important for this stage of the unit to have an information gap so that free practice can occur. When they have read the information, ask them to sit (or stand) at opposite sides of their table (the reception desk). Ask Student A to start the first dialogue: *Good afternoon. Welcome to the Sudari Hotel.* Go around the class, monitoring and supporting. Fast finishers can change roles, A and B. Strong students could introduce further realistic situations from their own experience, brief their partner and then role-play them, e.g. guests sometimes don't want to leave their passports at reception – they need them at the bank or want them with them when they go out; guests want to dine late; guests want a very early breakfast before departure.

Set up a 'reception desk' at the front of the room and ask pairs of students to perform their dialogues in front of the class.

■ More words to use

See Workbook page 15 for a wordbuilding exercise using some of the new words from the unit.

7 Dealing with check-in problems

> **Situations/functions**
> Finding solutions for problems
> Dealing with guests' special needs
>
> **Structures**
> Past Simple
> *have got/haven't got*

■ Revision of Unit 6

Expressions to learn

Ask students to look at the flow chart of check-in procedures from Unit 6 and to give you the receptionist's expressions for each stage.

New words to use

Make flashcards of the words (see Unit 2).

Other revision suggestions

- Write times on the board to check fluency of *a.m./ p.m.*, *in the morning/in the evening*, speaking the 24-hour clock.
- Get students to practise dialogues in pairs, reading the Listening script from Unit 6.
- Tell students to do one of the Activity role-plays from Unit 6, working with a different partner.

■ Starter

Ask students with work experience about check-in problems they have had in their hotels. Make a list on the board of common situations where guests have been unhappy. Look at the pictures and ask students to identify the three problem situations.

Answers

a car park full
b room isn't ready
c people at wrong hotel

■ Listening *Problems at check-in*

Most of the New words to use in this unit are actually from the second Listening. Check the context in which vocabulary from the first Listening is used and pre-teach: *complimentary, free, happen, occasionally, overbook, service* (see Introduction for suggestions). Give examples of the words in sentences in the same context and practise pronunciation of any difficult words so that students can identify them in the Listening.

1 ∩ **7.1** Tell students to read problem situations a–d. Play the recording and ask them to match the dialogues with the situations. Check answers around the class. Play the recording again with pauses for students to check their answers.

Answers

a 3 b 1 c 4 d 2

2 ∩ **7.1** Ask students to read sentences 1–8 and try to predict the missing words in pairs. Play the recording again and ask students to check their answers. Ask them to read the sentences aloud and check pronunciation, intonation and use of short forms.

Answers

1 isn't ready	5 've asked, for your room
2 you like	6 sent, confirmation
3 've reserved	7 not far
4 weeks ago	8 pre-book

3 Ask students to work with a partner to complete the receptionist's part of the dialogue. They could use Expressions to learn to help. Get students to practise speaking the dialogue. Go around the class, checking accuracy and polite intonation. Make sure that students change roles. Suggest that some students perform their dialogues in front of the class.

■ Language study

Expressions to learn

Ask students to read the expressions aloud. Check pronunciation and intonation. Ask students to learn the expressions for homework.

New words to use

Most of these words are from the second Listening so will be new to students. Elicit the words from around the class by giving students prompts (see Unit 2). Check pronunciation of any difficult words and get students to repeat after you individually and chorally. Ask students to learn the new words for homework.

Language check

Past Simple

Ask students to read the notes and examples. Check they can form the negative and question forms.

Ask students to complete the exercise. Refer lower-level students to the Irregular verbs list on page 111 of the Student's Book. Check answers around the class. Drill correct Past Simple forms of some verbs (using the list on page 111) if many mistakes are made. Ask students to study the list for homework.

Answers

> flew, slept, felt, got, thought, told, weren't, sat, had, went

have got/haven't got

Ask students to read the examples. Stress the importance of use for spoken English, but not for letter writing.

2 Divide the class into pairs, Student A and Student B. Direct them to their information. Read the example question and answer about the Crowne Plaza Hotel. Ask Student B to continue asking questions. Then change roles with Student A asking questions about the Sunset Beach Hotel. Go around the class, checking accuracy, pronunciation and intonation. Model and practise sentences where necessary.

■ Listening *Dealing with special needs*

Brainstorm a list of special needs that hotel guests may have. Encourage students to talk about situations from their own work experience and to consider other cultures, people with disabilities or needing special diets, children, women travelling alone. How sensitive are hotels to people's needs?

1 🎧 7.2 Ask students to read the categories. Play the recording and ask them to tick the three categories dealt with by the receptionist.

Answers

> disabled access, allergies, children's needs

2 🎧 7.2 Ask students if they can tell you the items requested in the three categories. Play the recording again and ask them to make a list.

Answers

> 1 room and bathroom with wheelchair access
> 2 smoke-free room, allergy-tested pillows
> 3 adjoining room, crib, high chair, children's menu, hot water for baby's bottle

3 Ask students around the class to make complete sentences using the request phrases. Refer them back to Expressions to learn for the receptionist's responses. Ask them to form pairs and practise requests and responses. Go around the class, checking and supporting. Make sure that each student uses a variety of request phrases, not just *I'd like … .*

■ Activity

Tell students they are going to deal with three guests' special needs, practising the language from the unit. Divide the class into pairs, Student A and Student B, and direct them to their roles. Ask them to read their roles and check any unfamiliar vocabulary. Tell them to work facing each other across the 'reception desk'. Student A starts the first dialogue: *Good morning. Can I help you?* Go around the class, monitoring and supporting.

Set up a 'reception desk' at the front of the room and ask pairs of students to perform their dialogues in front of the class.

■ More words to use

See Workbook page 17 for an exercise that extends on some of the new words from the unit.

8 Explaining how things work in the hotel room

Situations/functions
Helping guests with the room facilities
Small talk

Structures
Imperatives for instructions
Adjectives and adverbs

■ Revision of Unit 7

Expressions to learn

Elicit the expressions by asking students to respond to situations: *guests arrive before room is ready / elderly guests urgently need their room / hotel has overbooked / reception has no reservation in that name / car park is full.*

New words to use

Make flashcards of the words (see Unit 2).

Other revision suggestions

- Get students to practise dialogues in pairs, reading the Listening script from Unit 7.
- Divide the class into two, with books closed. Use the Irregular verbs list on page 111 of the Student's Book for a team game.
- Tell students to do one of the Activity role-plays from Unit 7, working with a different partner.

■ Starter

Ask students to look at the pictures and identify the problems the guests are having. Encourage students to tell stories from their work experience or to suggest other situations where guests might have problems with room facilities. Make a list on the board.

Answers

a	getting into the room
b	using the air conditioning
c	switching on the lights
d	using the safe deposit box
e	using the shower

■ Listening *How things work*

Pre-teach any remaining unfamiliar vocabulary from New words to use (see Introduction). Elicit the words using the pictures or any classroom equipment to hand.

1 🎧 8.1 The Listening covers the situations in the pictures so ask students to read sentences 1–8 and predict the correct alternatives. Play the recording so that they can check their answers.

Answers

1	key card
2	asks a porter
3	doesn't know how to make the lights work
4	leave the key card in
5	switched on
6	shower
7	after
8	the same

2 🎧 8.1 Ask students to read sentences 1–8 and try to predict the missing words in pairs. Play the recording again and ask students to check their answers. Ask them to read the sentences aloud and check pronunciation, intonation and use of short forms.

Answers

1 get into	5 on/off button
2 to work	6 pull up, on top of
3 've just got, lights work	7 enter, 4-digit
4 hot and, can't open	8 key in

Practise the Expressions to learn before doing exercise 3.

3 Look at the verbs in the boxes with the class. Mime the actions and ask students to give the verbs. Ask students to form pairs and to practise explaining how things work using the verbs. Refer them to the Listening script if they need help. Go around the class, checking accuracy and pronunciation. Make sure that students take turns to give instructions. Ask some students to explain the two scenarios in front of the class. Correct and practise any errors.

4 Ask students to choose one of the other problem situations from the list on the board. Ask them to work with a partner and practise explaining how to deal with the situation. Go around the class, helping and making sure that students take turns to explain.

■ Language study

Expressions to learn

Ask students to read the expressions aloud. Check pronunciation and intonation. Ask students to learn the expressions for homework.

New words to use

Elicit the words from around the class by giving students prompts (see Unit 2). Check pronunciation of any difficult words and get students to repeat after you individually and chorally. Ask students to learn the new words for homework.

Language check

Imperatives

Ask students to read the examples. Elicit more examples from the exercises they have just completed using *insert*, *key in*, *open*, etc.

1 Check that everyone understands the verbs in the box and then ask students to complete the exercise. Check answers around the class and ask two or three students to read the instructions aloud to the class. Correct and model pronunciation and intonation where necessary and ask the class to repeat after you.

Answers

1 Ask	3 Click on	5 Enter
2 Log on	4 Complete	

2 On the board, brainstorm a list of activities for which instructions are useful, in addition to the three activities given. Elicit verbs and write them next to the activities. Ask students to choose one activity and write a clear list of instructions for it. Ask students around the class to read their instructions aloud. Correct and model sentences where necessary, but be positive and constructive about students' work.

Adjectives and adverbs

Quickly go over the difference between adjectives (describe nouns: *a quiet room*) and adverbs (describe verbs: *she spoke quietly*). Ask for examples in sentences. Then ask students to read the examples in their books. Elicit examples of sentences using irregular adverbs. Note that adjectives ending in *y*, drop the *y* and add *-ily* to form adverbs: *happy/happily*. Students may query adverbs which exist but have different meanings from the adjective, e.g. *hardly*: *There are hardly any rooms left* (very few) / *She can hardly see* (almost not at all); *lately*: *Have you seen her lately?* (recently).

3 Ask students to complete the exercise. Check answers around the class.

Answers

1 easily	4 well	7 busy, slow
2 quickly	5 frequently	8 good
3 securely	6 separate	

■ Listening *Small talk*

Small talk often causes problems for learners, so it would be useful to spend some time on it now and to review at any point when there are a few minutes of class time left.

1 🎧 **8.2** Tell students to listen carefully to the receptionist's intonation and play the recording. Ask students to complete the exercise. Play the recording again with pauses, so they can check their answers.

Answers

1 c	2 f	3 a	4 h	5 i	6 b	7 e	8 g	9 d

2 🎧 **8.2** Ask students to practise the dialogues in pairs. Go around the class, monitoring and supporting. Play the recording again if necessary to emphasize the importance of correct intonation. Brainstorm other topics for small talk: journeys, where people come from, how they feel, how long they're staying, what they like doing, what there is to do, food, previous travel, family, jobs (all these may not be appropriate at check-in but are acceptable general conversation). Ask students with work experience to tell the class about situations they have found difficult. Model and practise sentences. Keep a note of all useful student input to recycle at a later date.

■ Activity

Tell students they are going to practise the language from the unit in two dialogues that include check-in, instructions on using key card and room facilities, and small talk. Divide the class into pairs, Student A and Student B, and direct them to their roles. Ask them to read their roles and check any unfamiliar vocabulary. For the first dialogue, ask students to work facing each other across the 'reception desk'. Student A starts the first dialogue: *Good evening. Would you like to check in?* The second dialogue is on the phone. Students should sit back to back. Student B starts: *Hello. How can I help?* Go around the class, monitoring and supporting. Ask some students to perform their dialogues in front of the class.

■ More words to use

Write these words on the board: *bright, cloudy, dull, foggy, freezing, rainy, sleeting, snowing, sunny, warm, wet, windy*. Tell students to look up any new words in the Glossary. Ask students to read the words aloud and check pronunciation.

9 Serving drinks

Situations/functions
Service in the bar and restaurant

Structures
Question form review

■ Revision of Unit 8

Expressions to learn

Elicit the expressions by asking students for instructions for hotel room facilities: *opening the door with the key card / activating the lights / switching on the air conditioning / operating the safe deposit box / changing from bath to shower.*

New words to use / More words to use

Make flashcards of the words (see Unit 2).

Other revision suggestions

- Write a list of adjectives from the Language check on the board. Point to an adjective, give a suitable noun or verb and ask students to form a sentence with either the adjective or its adverb equivalent as appropriate, e.g. *frequent – run: Buses run frequently to the city centre.*
- Get students to practise small talk, using the second Listening script from Unit 8. Encourage them to use other topics and weather words.
- Tell students to do the first Activity role-play from Unit 8, working with a different partner.

■ Starter

Find out if any students have worked in bars. What kind of drinks did they serve? What do students order when they go to bars? Look at the collage of drinks. Check if students are familiar with them. It will provide revision for students who have followed *Highly Recommended 1*. Ask about different types of drink: beer, wine, spirits and non-alcoholic drinks or mixers. The different types of beer often cause confusion: lager is a light-coloured beer popular all over the world and sold draught as well as in bottles and cans; bitter is a darker-coloured, less fizzy and stronger-tasting beer very popular in the UK. It is mainly sold draught, but is also exported in bottles and cans. Ask what the most popular drinks are in the different categories in students' countries and what the age limit is for buying alcohol (18 in Europe, 21 in the US). Ask students to work in pairs to put the words in

the box into one or more of the lists in the table. Check answers around the class and discuss any differences.

Answers

Beers:	draught, lager, bitter, light
Wines:	full-bodied, dry, sweet, red, white, medium, light, sparkling, rosé, magnum
Spirits:	dry (gin), white (rum), double, single
Non-alcoholic:	mixer, still, soft drink, sparkling, fizzy

■ Listening *A busy night in the bar*

Again ask about students' experience of working in bars. Have they ever had any problems with customers? What kinds of situations do bar staff have to deal with in bars and pubs all over the world? Pre-teach any remaining unfamiliar vocabulary from New words to use (see Introduction). Many of the words occur in the second Listening.

1 🎧 **9.1** Tell students they are going to hear bar staff deal with several situations during a busy night in a bar. Play the recording and ask students to read the questions. Offer to play the recording again before they give their answers. Check answers around the class.

Answers

1 A bottle of champagne, an ice bucket and six flutes.
2 They started a tab behind the bar.
3 Down the stairs on the right.
4 No – the waiter/waitress serves them.
5 They were very noisy – customers had complained.
6 She didn't look 18.

2 🎧 **9.1** Play the recording again and ask students to match the parts of the sentences. They are a mix of customer and staff sentences. Stronger students can do the matching before listening again. Ask them to read the sentences aloud and check pronunciation and intonation.

Answers

1 c 2 e 3 h 4 f 5 g 6 b 7 a 8 d

3 Ask students to work in pairs. They should use the prompts and the sentences in exercise 2 to practise expressions for situations in the bar. Go around the class, checking accuracy and pronunciation.

22 | Unit 9 Serving drinks

Language study

Expressions to learn

Ask students to read the expressions aloud. Check pronunciation and intonation. Ask students to learn the expressions for homework.

New words to use

Elicit the words from around the class by giving students prompts (see Unit 2). Check pronunciation of any difficult words and get students to repeat after you individually and chorally. Ask students to learn the new words for homework.

Language check

Question forms

This is a revision of word order in questions. Read through the question types one at a time and elicit more examples. Give some help on the board:

Yes/no *questions using auxiliary verbs and modals: is/ was/do/did/have/will/can/could/would*

Wh- *questions using: what/when/where/who/ whose/ which/why/how*

Subject *questions using: who/what*

Prepositions in Wh- *questions: Who's it for? What's it about? Why's it outside?*

1 Ask students to complete the exercise. Check answers around the class.

Answers

1 Can you ask them to calm down?
2 What did the under-age drinkers order?
3 What other soft drinks have you got?
4 Who broke the glass on the terrace?
5 Did the men leave the bar quietly?
6 What drinks did table 3 ask for?
7 Have you removed the glass from the terrace?
8 Who wants to start a tab behind the bar?

2 Ask students to work in pairs to make questions. Check answers and ask students to practise speaking the mini-dialogues.

Answers

1 Did you check their ID?
2 Where did the waiter take the ice bucket?
3 Who is Mario working with?
4 Is the young Australian waiter good at his job?
5 What time do you finish work?
6 Who ordered champagne?
7 Would you like citrus or pineapple?
8 Who refused to serve you?

■ Listening *Drinks at the table*

Find out if any students have served drinks in a restaurant. Ask what drinks are usually served before, during and after a meal. Get students to suggest different aperitifs, wines and liqueurs. Elicit vocabulary by asking what they know about wine: *How is red/white wine served?* (red – room temperature, white – chilled). *What do we call wine that has been kept too long or not stored well?* (corked).

1 ⌒ 9.2 Ask students to read the questions. Play the recording. Check answers around the class.

Answers

1 Italy	3 a bottle of Bordeaux	5 a half-bottle
2 full-bodied	4 It's corked	

2 ⌒ 9.2 Ask students to look at the Drinks list (note that *cl* = *centilitres* – 70 cl is the wine bottle size). Play the recording again and ask students to tick the drinks ordered. Check answers around the class.

Answers

glass of house white, whisky sour, bottle of Bordeaux, half-bottle of Royal Tokaji, Grand Marnier, Highland Park (single malt)

3 Model any pronunciation difficulties with the drinks and get students to repeat after you. Ask students to work in pairs offering and ordering drinks. Go around the class, monitoring and helping.

■ Activity

Tell students they are going to take turns ordering drinks in a bar, practising the language from the unit. Divide the class into customers and servers and ask them to read their information. Direct them to the Drinks list on page 62. For more realism, you could make photocopies of the list for each student. Refer slow starters to the example sentences. Go around the class, monitoring and supporting. Remind students to change roles. Ask some students to perform their dialogues in front of the class.

■ More words to use

Write these words on the board: *sommelier, cork, corkscrew, breathe, plastic, screw top, chambrer, vintage, sediment.* Tell students to look up any new words in the Glossary. Ask students to read the words aloud and check pronunciation.

Situations/functions
Taking customers' orders
Explaining menus and dishes
Talking about cheeses and coffee

Structures
Talking about quantity

■ Revision of Unit 9

Expressions to learn

Elicit the expressions by giving situations: *a customer doesn't want to pay for the drinks until the end of the evening / a waiter checks which table ordered champagne / a customer wants directions to the toilets / a server requests the customer's ID*, etc.

New words to use / More words to use

Make flashcards of the words including those from the Starter. This is a good unit to make a team game out of vocabulary revision (see Revision of Unit 2).

Other revision suggestions

- Ask for examples of different question forms. Give prompts on the board: *do/did*; *is/can/would*; *what can/when is/where did*; *who/what* as subjects.
- Get students to practise the second Listening script from Unit 9 in groups of three.
- Tell students to do the Activity from Unit 9, working with a different partner.

■ Starter

Ask students about their own experience of working in restaurants. What kind of menus have they served? Look at the menu together and teach unfamiliar vocabulary before students do the Starter tasks. Tell students to keep their ordered menus to use in exercises 1 and 3. Goat's cheese and red onion tart is usually on a menu as a starter but sometimes as a main course vegetarian option. Encourage students to talk about national dishes/favourite dishes. Write translations on the board of popular dishes and ingredients.

■ Listening *Are you ready to order?*

Ask students for any stories they may have from their work experience. Have they had any awkward or very fussy customers? Pre-teach any remaining unfamiliar vocabulary from New words to use (see Introduction).

The first Listening deals with starter and main course orders.

1 🎧 **10.1** Play the recording and ask students to tick the items ordered. Play the recording again with pauses for students to check their answers or check answers around the class.

Answers

Starters:	Soup of the day, Goat's cheese and red onion tart.
Main courses:	Mushroom risotto, Sea bass with spicy mango salsa.

2 🎧 **10.1** Ask students to work in pairs and try to complete the sentences before listening to the recording again. Check answers around the class.

Answers

1 soup of the day	5 made from, some
2 any nuts	6 another bottle
3 consists of, different types	7 finished
4 very popular	8 dessert menu

Ask students to read the Expressions to learn. Get them to give further examples (using dishes that they know) in sentences with *contains/doesn't contain, made from, consists of*. Also teach and practise other useful expressions: *served with, cooked in, mixed with*.

3 Check that students know how to explain the items on the menu. Divide the class into groups of three: pairs of diners and a server. If you have time and space, you could move the furniture around to create a restaurant scene and borrow some trays and dishes from the canteen. The server begins the role-play: *Are you ready to order?* Remind students to change roles when they've finished. Go around the class, monitoring accuracy, pronunciation and intonation. Note any common errors. Model corrections and get students to repeat after you where necessary.

■ Language study

Expressions to learn

Ask students to read the expressions aloud. Check pronunciation and intonation. Ask students to learn the expressions for homework.

New words to use

Elicit the words from around the class by giving students prompts (see Unit 2). Give a context for the words they haven't met yet: *compote*, *stewed* (fruit dessert), *frothy* (cappuccino coffee), *pistachio* (nut-flavoured ice cream). Check pronunciation of any difficult words and get students to repeat after you individually and chorally. Ask students to learn the new words for homework.

Language check

Talking about quantity

This is a revision of quantity words and countable/uncountable nouns. Read through the examples together. Ask students why we can't say *Another bread, please* (because *bread* is an uncountable noun). Brainstorm a list of uncountable nouns and write them on the board: food and drink items, articles of clothing (e.g. *trousers*, *shorts*, *pants*) and common mistakes (e.g. *information*, *equipment*). Read the examples of quantity words with countable and uncountable nouns. Remind students that to make an uncountable noun countable, add phrases like: *a slice (of bread)*, *a piece (of meat)*, *a bottle (of wine)*. Ask students to complete the exercise, using each word or phrase in the box just once. Check answers around the class.

Answers

1 many	4 How much, more
2 How many, few, enough	5 a little
3 much	6 another, some

■ Listening *Dessert and coffee*

Ask students about their favourite desserts and the types of coffee they drink. If any students work in a restaurant, find out what desserts they serve and which are the most popular. Ask if there is a difference between coffees that locals and tourists order. Look at the pictures together and elicit the vocabulary.

1 🎧 **10.2** Play the recording and ask students to note down what the family ordered. Check answers around the class.

Answers

mango sorbet, chocolate and pistachio ice cream, fruit compote with cream, a selection of cheeses (a little Dolcelatte, a slice of Brie and a slice of Manchego), one Americano, one latte, one espresso, one cappuccino

2 🎧 **10.2** Play the recording again and ask students to underline the correct alternative. Stronger or more experienced students will be able to do this without listening again. Check answers around the class. Ask students to read the sentences aloud and correct and model pronunciation where necessary. Get students to repeat after you individually and chorally.

Answers

1 water ice	5 regular
2 stewed	6 milky
3 creamy	7 strong
4 strong	8 frothy

3 Ask students to work in pairs to practise asking and answering about the different desserts, cheeses and coffees. Make sure they take turns to be server and customer. Go around the class, monitoring and helping.

■ Activity

For students training in restaurant service and cuisine, it will be worth spending some time consolidating and extending the contents of this unit with students' own contributions. You could set a homework task for students to research ingredients and dishes for a three-course menu from their own region. Get students to write their suggestions on the board and discuss the ingredients or special features of each dish.

Next ask students to work in pairs and write a menu with choices from the options on the board, ready to give to their 'customer'. Give them time to practise explaining the dishes to each other.

Then ask students to work with a different partner and take turns ordering from each other's menu. Remind them to ask and answer questions about what the dishes consist of, etc. Go around the class, monitoring and supporting. Ask two or three pairs to perform their dialogues in front of the class.

■ More words to use

Write these words on the board: *beat*, *mash*, *stir*, *chop*, *julienne*. Tell students to look up any new words in the Glossary. Ask students to read the words aloud and check pronunciation.

11 Know your region

⟐ **Situations/functions**
Giving information on visitor attractions
Advising guests on what to do

⟐ **Structures**
Comparisons: *-er than*, *the -est*; *more/the most*;
(not) as ... as, not so ... as

■ Revision of Unit 10

Expressions to learn

Write *contains*, *made from* and *consists of* on the board. Elicit the expressions by giving prompts of dishes which students know. Elicit other expressions by getting students to do the following: Ask for a main course recommendation. / Recommend the fish. / Check the customer is happy with their meal. / Ask for more of the same wine. / Ask for more bread. / Tell the customer you'll bring more bread.

New words to use / More words to use

Make flashcards of the words including those from menus that students have contributed. This is also a good unit to make a team game out of vocabulary revision (see Revision of Unit 2).

Other revision suggestions

- Get students to practise dialogues in groups of three, reading the Listening scripts from Unit 10.
- Tell students to do the Activity from Unit 10, working with a different partner. They could use the menu from the Starter in the unit.

■ Starter

Point out to students that the tourist industry is the biggest industry in the world, in terms of number of people employed. Their future jobs in hospitality depend on the industry. It is essential for personnel who have direct contact with customers to know about the tourist industry in their region, so they can promote the different attractions and be informative and customer-oriented. Ask students to make a general list of visitor attractions. Tell them to look at the pictures to help. Then ask what they think the main visitor attractions are in their region. Translate as closely as possible and write the attractions on the board (students could find an English website if facilities are available). Keep this information for exercise 3 and the Activity.

■ Listening *Advising tourists*

Pre-teach any unfamiliar vocabulary from New words to use (see Introduction). Practise the pronunciation of difficult words, e.g. *archaeology*, *architecture*, *definitely*.

1 ⊙ **11.1** Tell students to look at their lists of visitor attractions. Play the recording and ask them to tick the attractions they hear and to add any attractions not already on their lists. Tell them to compare lists with a partner and then check answers around the class.

Answers

concerts, theatre, opera, museums (Folk, Local History and National), art gallery, cathedral, churches, history walks, restaurants, bars, park

2 ⊙ **11.1** Play the recording again and ask students to complete the sentences. Check answers orally around the class. This would be a good point to look at the Language check and revise or teach comparative and superlative forms. Refer back to the relevant sentences in exercise 2, asking students to underline the comparative and superlative forms, e.g. *more expensive than*.

Answers

1 you recommend	5 up to date
2 opera, theatre	6 most interesting
3 ask the concierge	7 so old, certainly
4 traditional than	8 best area

Practise the Expressions to learn before doing exercise 3.

3 Tell students to look back at their lists from the Starter, plus any information on the board about local attractions. Brainstorm any more local or regional information and write it on the board. Tell students to use the sentences in exercise 2 and Expressions to learn to help them ask and answer questions about attractions.

■ Language study

Expressions to learn

Ask students to read the expressions aloud, completing unfinished ones with their own information. Check pronunciation and intonation. Ask students to learn the expressions for homework.

New words to use

Elicit the words from around the class by giving students prompts (see Unit 2). Check pronunciation of any difficult words and get students to repeat after you individually and chorally. Ask students to learn the new words for homework.

Language check

Comparisons

Read the examples with the class, highlighting the comparative and superlative forms. Point out that the comparative form of the adjective is not used with *(not) as … as* and *(not) so … as*.

1 Ask students to turn to the Listening script on page 73 and complete the list of 14 comparative and superlative forms. Check answers orally around the class.

Answers

3 more traditional than	10 the oldest
4 more up to date	11 more informative than
6 the longest	12 further
7 the best	13 as good as
8 not so old as	14 cheaper
9 more beautiful	

2 Tell students to double check the irregular adjectives in the Language check. Also remind them that adjectives ending in *y*, drop the *y* and add *ier/iest* in the comparative and superlative forms, e.g. *happier/happiest*. Ask students to complete the sentences. Check answers around the class.

Answers

1 more expensive	5 worse
2 the oldest	6 the least
3 busier	7 better
4 cold as	8 not so frequent

■ **Listening** *Things to do in Granada*

Check if students know anything about Granada. Tell them a little about the place: old city in southern Spain surrounded by mountains; full of Moorish, Islamic, and Christian history and architecture; the citadel of the Alhambra is its 'jewel'.

1 🎧 **11.2** Play the recording and ask students to number the places in order.

Answers

a 3 b 1 c 4 d 5 e 2

Ask if there were any difficulties with vocabulary. *Tapas* are a traditional way of eating in Spain – small bowls of all kinds of different foods shared by diners. *Flamenco* is a traditional way of dancing from southern Spain – very vibrant with tapping heels, castanets and swirling skirts. *Islamic culture* in the Alhambra is seen in the design and purpose of the buildings, the artwork and designs on the walls and ceilings, the poetry and writings, the stories of the people who lived there.

2 🎧 **11.2** Play the recording again. Ask students to write their answers next to the places in exercise 1. Check answers around the class.

Answers

a shopping, museums
b gardens, architecture, history, Islamic culture
c flamenco
d hiking
e tapas bars, architecture, shopping, history

3 As an alternative to Granada, students could focus on a tourist attraction in their region. They may need to do some research first though. This could be combined with further research for a more comprehensive picture of tourism in the area for the Activity role-play.

■ **Activity**

As an alternative to using the information on New York and Istanbul, this unit provides a good opportunity to continue talking about students' own region by setting students a project to find out about tourist attractions in the area. Ask students to visit tourist offices, hotels, local attractions, libraries and websites, and to put together a guide leaflet for the area. They can use the information as a basis for the Activity role-play. While students are doing the role-play, go around the class, monitoring and supporting. Ask some students to perform their dialogues or alternatively to present their research in front of the class.

■ **More words to use**

Write these words on the board: *skyscraper, temple, mosque, waterfront, well, minaret, dome, courtyard*. Tell students to look up any new words in the Glossary. Ask students to read the words aloud and check pronunciation.

12 Explaining travel options

▪ **Situations/functions**
Talking to guests about travel options
Giving advice about local transport and tickets

▪ **Structures**
Recommending, suggesting and advising

▪ Revision of Unit 11

Expressions to learn

Ask for suggestions of visitor attractions using starter phrases like: *What about ...? / I think ... / Another thing ... / The main areas ...* . Ask students to compare different places or attractions using comparative and superlative forms. Give prompts where necessary, e.g. Paris vs Marseilles, St Michael's church vs St Stephen's. Elicit *not so ... as, as ... as* forms and irregular adjectives.

New words to use / More words to use

Make flashcards of the words (see Unit 2). You could also include vocabulary development arising from students' research of local attractions.

Other revision suggestions

- Get students to practise dialogues in pairs, reading the Listening scripts from Unit 11.
- Ask for volunteers to present a short overview of visitor attractions in your area to the class.

▪ Starter

1 Front-office staff are often asked about the best way to get to places. Look at the pictures of the different forms of transport and ask students to name them. Make a list on the board. Ask if they can add any more to the list. Find out which forms of transport are available where they live.

Answers

a tram	e cable car	i taxi
b ferry	f bus	j minibus
c underground train	g plane	
d pedicab	h monorail train	

2 Open a discussion on public transport. What transport do students use? How often? What do they prefer? Why? How does the fare system work? What about in the nearest city? Encourage students to think of the advantages and disadvantages of different forms of

transport in their city/region. Which are the quickest, most convenient, most comfortable, least expensive, etc? Which would be the most enjoyable for tourists to use and why?

▪ Listening *Giving advice about local trave*

Pre-teach any remaining unfamiliar vocabulary from New words to use (see Introduction). Some of the words are from the second Listening but relate to the information and suggestions that students will have given in the Starter.

1 🎧 **12.1** Tell students they are going to hear three different enquiries about ways to travel. Play the recording and ask students to complete the guests' notes. Tell them to compare notes with a partner. For lower-level students, look at the incomplete notes first. Then play the dialogues one at a time and complete the notes. Play the recording again with pauses between the dialogues and check answers around the class.

Answers

1 9.30	6 14	10 three
2 market square	7 Central Station	11 train
3 6.00	8 three	12 underground
4 packed lunch	9 five	13 (river)boat
5 underground		

2 🎧 **12.1** Ask students to read the sentence parts and match them to make sentences. For lower-level students, play the recording again in sections and give them time to find the answers. Play the recording again with pauses and ask students to check their answers. Get students around the class to read the sentences aloud.

Answers

1 d	2 g	3 a	4 h	5 c	6 e	7 i	8 f	9 b

3 This is an opportunity to consolidate the language already used. Read the Expressions to learn together, completing any unfinished sentences with information from the Listening. The receptionist's responses are in the same order as in the previous exercise. The guest begins each dialogue: *Could you tell us how to get to ...?*

Unit 12 Explaining travel options

Language study

Expressions to learn

Ask students to read the expressions aloud, completing any unfinished ones with their own information. Check pronunciation and intonation. Ask students to learn the expressions for homework.

New words to use

Elicit the words from around the class by giving students prompts (see Unit 2). Check the pronunciation of any difficult words and get students to repeat after you individually and chorally. Ask students to learn the new words for homework.

Language check

Recommending, suggesting and advising

Present these as expressions to use for suggesting, recommending and advising. Do not attempt a grammatical analysis. Write the expressions on the board and then drill them around the class by pointing to an expression and giving a form of transport. Students can continue drilling each other in pairs. Then ask students to complete the exercise by underlining the correct alternative. Correct orally around the class.

Answers

1 to visit	4 buying	7 to rent
2 take	5 go	8 visiting
3 to see	6 take	

■ Listening *Giving advice about tickets*

1   Ask students to discuss the transport payment systems they are familiar with in small groups. Some may have experience of travel in different cities or countries. Ask groups to report back to the whole class. Elicit the vocabulary in New words that was not used in the first Listening.

2   🎧 **12.2** Depending on the language level of your class, play the dialogues one by one or altogether. Ask students to note the forms of transport discussed. Check answers around the class.

Answers

1 ferry	3 MTR (metro system)
2 bus	4 U-bahn, ferries

3   🎧 **12.2** Ask students to read the questions and discuss them with a partner, writing down what they think the answers are. Play the recording again and ask students to check their answers. Check answers orally around the class.

Answers

1 get tickets in advance
2 the ticket machine at the bus stop
3 $150
4 yes
5 three years
6 travel card
7 to get passport photos and buy the card
8 The price depends on how long you want the card for and the number of zones it covers.

4   You could let lower-level students read the Listening script with a partner before practising with just the prompts. Start students off with a few phrases on the board: *Where can I buy … ? I'd recommend getting … .* Stronger students could adapt the prompts to give advice about tickets and travel in their own region or city.

■ Activity

Tell students they are going to practise giving advice about travel and tickets. Divide the class into pairs, Student A and Student B. Pair stronger with weaker students if you have a mixed-level class. Direct students to their roles. As they read their roles, go around the class and help with any queries. Ask Student A to start the first dialogue: *Can you tell me how to get to …?* Go around the class, monitoring and supporting. Ask some students to perform their dialogues in front of the class.

In addition (or alternatively), students could make a list of attractions that tourists visit in their town or city. Ask them to choose one attraction each and decide how they would advise a visitor to get there from a certain point (e.g. the college, the railway station, a hotel). What sort of transport would they recommend and what would be the best type of ticket? Then students work in pairs to ask for and give advice about travel and tickets.

■ More words to use

Write these words on the board: *concourse, change (trains), tram, pier, travel card, route, funicular, monorail, minibus*. Tell students to look up any new words in the Glossary. Ask students to read the words aloud and check pronunciation.

13 Giving directions

> **Situations/functions**
> Giving directions inside and outside the hotel
>
> **Structures**
> Prepositions of direction

■ Revision of Unit 12

Expressions to learn

Review the language of recommending, suggesting and advising. Write some starter phrases on the board: *Why don't you …? / You could … / Why not …?* Ask students for more examples from the expressions they have studied. Give them a form of transport and a place in turn, and ask them to use an expression on the board to make a sentence, e.g. *tram/concert hall – You could take the tram to the concert hall.* Review the language of transport payment systems by asking about students' own knowledge or experience of buying tickets and how they are used.

New words to use / More words to use

Make flashcards of the words (see Unit 2). Include all new transport vocabulary that came up in the unit.

Other revision suggestions

- Get students to practise dialogues in pairs, reading the Listening scripts from Unit 12.
- Tell students to do the Activity from Unit 12, working with a different partner.

■ Starter

Ask students to work with a partner and discuss what the icons at the top of the hotel plan represent. Check answers around the class.

Answers

1 lift	3 fitness centre	5 conference centre
2 toilets	4 swimming pool	6 garden

■ Listening *Giving directions inside the hotel*

1 🎧 **13.1** Ask students to look at the plan. The information in the Listening will indicate where the icons they have just discussed go on the plan. Play the recording. Students match the icons to the places.

Answers

a 4	b 3	c 1	d 5	e 2	f 6

2 🎧 **13.1** Ask students to try and complete the sentences before listening to the recording again. Play the recording again and ask students to check their sentences. Check answers orally around the class.

Answers

1 walk across
2 to get to
3 down, along, the right
4 walk through, to, take
5 continue along, take
6 out onto
7 straight on, to
8 come out, on the

3 Ask students to read the Expressions to learn. Point out the use of the imperative in some of the sentences. Remind students about the imperative in their instruction-giving in Unit 8 (*push the button*, *insert the card*, etc.). They can use the hotel plan, exercise 2 and the expressions to ask for and give directions. Go around the class, monitoring and supporting where necessary.

■ Language study

Expressions to learn

Ask students to read the expressions aloud, completing any unfinished ones with their own information. Check pronunciation and intonation. Ask students to learn the expressions for homework.

New words to use

Elicit the words from around the class by giving students prompts (see Introduction). Note that *hall* is often used instead of *corridor*: *The entrance is down the hall. Lobby* is the same as *reception area*. Check pronunciation of any difficult words and get students to repeat after you individually and chorally. Ask students to learn the new words for homework.

Language check
Prepositions of direction

Ask students to look at the preposition diagrams. Get them to describe the meaning of the prepositions by miming, explaining or giving a clear example sentence, e.g. *Chef went into the kitchen. We walked along the river bank.* Then ask students to complete the exercise. Check answers around the class, using the hotel plan on page 28 to illustrate the correct prepositions if necessary.

Answers

1 past	5 on
2 round	6 into
3 along	7 through
4 to	8 out of

■ Listening *Giving directions to places outside the hotel*

1 🎧 **13.2** Ask students to look at the map at the bottom of the page. Tell them that they are going to hear directions from the hotel (ask them to find this on the map) to four different places of interest. Play the recording and ask students to follow the directions and find the places on the map. With lower-level students, you can play the directions one at a time with pauses and repeats as necessary.

Answers

1 art gallery	3 windmill
2 lighthouse	4 castle

2 🎧 **13.2** Ask students to read the sentences. Tell them that there is one piece of false information in each sentence. Then play the recording again and ask students to correct the false information. Ask students to compare with a partner before checking answers around the class.

Answers

1 There are art shops and tearooms in High Street.
2 You can see the river from the top of the art gallery.
3 The school is a new building.
4 You should leave your car in the car park.
5 You can walk from the library to the windmill.
6 The old cottages are on the left.

■ Activity

Tell students they are going to use the hotel plan and the map in the unit to practise giving directions. Divide the class into pairs, Student A and Student B, and direct them to their roles. Ask students to choose a partner. Refer weaker students back to exercise 2 in the first Listening and Expressions to learn if they need help.

Student A starts the first dialogue: *Can you tell me where the lifts are, please?* Go around the class, monitoring and supporting. Ask some students to perform their dialogues in front of the class.

Alternatively, instead of using the hotel plan and map in the Student's Book, ask students to take turns to give each other directions to places in the building they are in. Give stronger students maps of the city or town where they live and ask them to practise giving directions to places of interest.

■ More words to use

Write these words on the board: *cottage, windmill, art shop, wide, tearoom, lantern, narrow, wind turbine.* Tell students to look up any new words in the Glossary. Ask students to read the words aloud and check pronunciation.

Meeting customer needs

Situations/functions
Dealing with customer needs
Customer care and customer service
Structures
need/don't need, need doing, need to do

■ Revision of Unit 13

Expressions to learn

Ask students to tell you how to get to places in the building you are in. Continue with requests for directions to places in your town or local area. Use any city maps or plans you have used before with students. Write the prepositions of direction on the board and tell students to include them in their directions.

New words to use / More words to use

Make flashcards of the words (see Unit 2).

Other revision suggestion

• Get students to practise dialogues in pairs, reading the first Listening script from Unit 13.

■ Starter

Introduce the topic of customer care. Brainstorm the things that customers care about when staying in a hotel: clean rooms, pleasant reception service, efficient check-in and checkout, good food. Then ask students to think about the particular needs of customers. Ask them to look at the pictures and work with a partner to list the eight specific needs and requests suggested. Ask stronger students to help with vocabulary. This should provide revision for those who have used *Highly Recommended 1*.

Answers

a laundry/dry cleaning/pressing/ironing service
b directions to hotel
c taxi booking
d fresh towels
e mending service
f extra pillow
g wake-up call
h babysitting

Ask students to add to the list from their own knowledge and work experience. Elicit the type of special events or family parties that hotels host (e.g. weddings, wedding anniversaries, birthdays, retirement parties, funeral wakes). Ask about any very unusual requests students with work experience may have had. Help with vocabulary where necessary.

■ Listening *We're here to help you*

Pre-teach unfamiliar vocabulary from New words to use (see Introduction). Some of the words are from the second Listening and are quite challenging for students. Give the contexts in which they occur in the Listening now. They can be reviewed again before the second Listening: *budget* hotels are often 2-star for customers with a limited income or *budget*; a hotel should try *to exceed customer expectations* (a marketing phrase to learn); a *satisfied* customer will possibly come back and will certainly recommend a hotel or restaurant; a *successful* business makes a profit and has a good working atmosphere for employees and customers.

1 🎧 **14.1** The first Listening consists of three dialogues. Tell students to read the information in the Reason column. Then play the recording, with pauses if necessary, and ask students to complete what the customers need. Check answers around the class.

Answers

1 wake-up call (5.00), babysitter this evening
2 directions, (car park) card
3 pressing service, fresh towels

2 🎧 **14.1** Ask students to read sentences 1–9 and try to complete the gaps. Play the recording again in sections and ask students to check their answers. Get students to read the sentences aloud around the class.

Answers

1 some more	4 directions to	7 party, pressing
2 to put	5 parking permit	8 with you
3 we've someone	6 anything else	9 dropped them

Practise the Expressions to learn before doing exercise 3.

3 Students should take turns to be customer (A) and receptionist (B). Tell students to imagine that they are taking requests from guests either face to face or over the telephone. A reads the sentence as it is in the Student's Book and B responds helpfully. When they have completed the six responses, they can repeat, changing their A/B roles for the sentences.

Language study

Expressions to learn

Ask students to read the expressions aloud. Check pronunciation and intonation. Ask students to learn the expressions for homework.

New words to use

Elicit the words from around the class by giving students prompts (see Unit 1). Some of the more difficult words will be easier for students to remember if they learn them in phrases (collocations). Teach: *exceed expectations, improve service, satisfied customer, successful business*. Check the pronunciation of any difficult words and get students to repeat after you. Ask students to learn the new words for homework.

Language check

need

Ask students to read the examples of *need* meaning 'require' followed by either a noun or a verb in the *-ing* form. Get them to give you more examples from their own lives. Note that the opposite of *need* is *don't need*. *Needn't* is used in a completely different context, meaning there is no obligation (see Unit 21). Continue by looking at *need* meaning 'have to' followed by *to +* infinitive. Elicit more examples. Then ask students to complete the exercise. Check answers around the class.

Answers

1 need to book	5 Do they need
2 needs ... pressing	6 need cleaning
3 need to get	7 need to work
4 doesn't need	8 need

Listening *Customer care and customer service*

Reintroduce the concept of customer care. Ask students what it involves: looking after your customer; responding to their needs; keeping them satisfied/ happy. Ask if anyone can tell the class about different levels of service in hotels, e.g. the difference between a 2-star and a 5-star hotel.

1 🎧 **14.2** Ask students to read sentences 1–8. Play the recording and ask them to underline the correct alternative. Play the recording again with pauses and ask them to check their answers.

Answers

1 customer	4 porter	7 satisfied
2 exceed	5 Leisure	8 recommend
3 improve	6 specific	

2 🎧 **14.2** Stress again the importance of learning words in groups – it's much easier to remember. Stronger students will probably be able to do the matching without listening to the recording again. Check answers around the class.

Answers

1 b	2 f	3 g	4 h	5 a	6 e	7 c	8 d

3 Ask students to research in advance how the hotel star system works in their country. In the lesson, ask students to work with a partner to list services according to the system. Make a master list on the board of the different services under the star system. As an extra activity, give an example of a 2-star hotel in your area with a list of its services (or make one up or give a website). Ask students to work with a partner to make a list of suggestions to upgrade the hotel to 4-star (i.e. to improve the level of services, especially for customers with specific needs).

Activity

The Activity combines the special events referred to in the Starter with customer needs and practises the language of the unit. Divide the class into pairs, Student A and Student B, and direct them to their roles. As students read their roles, go around the class answering any queries. Ask students to sit back to back with a partner to simulate the telephone conversation. Student A begins the first dialogue: *Good afternoon. How can I help you?* Go around the class, monitoring and supporting. Ask some students to perform their dialogues in front of the class.

Alternatively, the 'customers' can make their own list of requirements for their special event (B1 wedding reception, A2 birthday party) and then make the phone calls.

More words to use

See Workbook page 31 for a vocabulary extension exercise based on a reading text.

Complaints and apologies

⇨ **Situations/functions**
Acknowledging and apologizing
Promising action

⇨ **Structures**
Present Perfect with *already*, *yet*, *just*, *for* and *since*

■ Revision of Unit 14

Expressions to learn

To elicit the expressions, tell students you are a hotel guest. Give requests to respond to: *more toiletries / clean towels / wake-up call / babysitter / directions to hotel / need for parking permit.*

New words to use

Make flashcards of the words, including the needs and requests brainstormed. If you have enough words, make a team game (see Revision of Unit 2). Practise the collocations from the second Listening. Give the first part of the phrase and elicit the second, e.g. *a satisfied (customer).*

Other revision suggestions

- Practise the use of *need* by eliciting the things a hotel should ask a customer who wants to hold a special event (wedding reception, child's party, funeral wake). Get students to tell you when the customer needs to pay the deposit, confirm numbers, decide on menus, etc.
- Get students to practise dialogues in pairs, reading the first Listening script from Unit 14.

■ Starter

Ask students who have worked to tell the class about their experience of customers complaining. How did they handle these situations? What are the usual options (apologize and put right; apologize and suggest something constructive if the situation is not in your control, e.g. rooms not ready; call the duty manager or your supervisor to deal with it)? Don't let this discussion go on too long! Tell students there will be more opportunity to talk about their experiences later.

Ask students to work in pairs to make a list of common complaints in hotels and restaurants. Compare as a class.

■ Listening *This is unacceptable*

Pre-teach unfamiliar vocabulary from New words to use (see Introduction).

1 🎧 **15.1** Ask students to read sentences 1–6. Play the recording and ask them to underline the correct alternative. Check answers around the class.

Answers

1 two	3 15 hours	5 ground
2 hasn't	4 changeover	6 late lunch

2 🎧 **15.1** Tell students to read sentences 1–8. Stronger students may be able to complete them without listening again. Play the recording again and ask students to complete/check the sentences. Check answers around the class.

Answers

1 servicing	5 page, duty
2 already had	6 complain about
3 three-hour, transfer	7 transferred us, information
4 be ready	8 have to

Ask students to look at the picture. The customer is obviously upset about something. Discuss the importance of good listening skills. You may not be able to do something about a problem, but the customer will always appreciate a sympathetic listener. Elicit how we show that we are listening actively (look at the person speaking, nod head, use expressions like *Mmm, Yes, Right, I see, Of course*).

3 Ask students to read the six steps and put them in order. Check the order around the class. Discussion of the order is fine. There isn't really a completely right or wrong answer as it depends on the conversation (a, c and e could be in a different order). Refer weaker students to the Expressions to learn to help find an expression to go with each step or let them listen to the recording again.

Model answers

a	2	I'm very sorry that you've had to wait.
b	6	I'll speak to housekeeping straightaway.
c	3	Mmm. Right.
d	1	What seems to be the problem?
e	4	That's not good. You're quite right.
f	5	I do understand.

4 Ask students to read the Manager/Guest roles and to practise dialogues using the language from exercise 2 and Expressions to learn. Make sure they change roles. Go around the class, supporting where necessary.

Language study

Expressions to learn

Ask students to read the expressions aloud. Check pronunciation and intonation, especially those expressions requiring a sympathetic tone of voice. Ask students to learn the expressions for homework.

New words to use

Elicit the words from around the class by giving students prompts (see Unit 1). Check pronunciation of any difficult words and get students to repeat after you. Ask students to learn the new words for homework.

Language check

Present Perfect

Read the uses of the Present Perfect. Ask students to match each example with the correct use. With weaker students, you may need to write the notes on the board and give more examples.

1 Read the prompts and the example answers. Tell students to complete the exercise. Check answers around the class.

Answers

> 3 The guests have already completed the registration cards.
> 4 They haven't booked a table for dinner yet.
> 5 The porter has just taken the luggage to room 43.
> 6 Mr and Mrs Laval haven't had their lunch yet.
> 7 He's just called to say they'll be late.
> 8 The guest has already talked to the tour rep.

for and *since*

Read the notes and examples with the class. Contrast *for* + period of time (*two weeks, three days, ten years, five minutes*) with *since* + particular time or date (*last week, 2008, Tuesday, eight o'clock*). Ask students to give example sentences about how long they have: lived here, studied English, worked in the hotel, been able to drive, etc. Get them to give alternative sentences using *for* and *since*.

2 Ask students to complete the exercise. Check answers around the class.

Answers

> 1 've had, for
> 2 haven't seen, since
> 3 's had, for
> 4 hasn't changed, since
> 5 has been, for

Listening *I'm really very sorry*

Stress the importance of looking at the person with the complaint and using the right intonation in the apology. It can seem rude if this is not done correctly.

1 🎧 **15.2** Ask students to read the complaints and apologies. Check for any unfamiliar vocabulary. Stronger students will be able to match the sentences before listening. Play the recording and get students to match or check the complaints and apologies. Check answers around the class.

Answers

> 1 f 2 g 3 b 4 c 5 h 6 d 7 a 8 e

2 Divide the class into Student A (complaining customer) and B (receptionist). You could play the dialogues again and ask students to repeat their parts, imitating the intonation on the recording. Change roles and play the recording again. Tell students to practise the dialogues in pairs. You could make the exercise fun by putting the sentences on cards so that each student has at least one complaint and a different apology. One student starts by reading their complaint (encourage them to exaggerate their intonation). The student with the correct apology responds. Receptionists must always sound apologetic and helpful however they are spoken to.

Activity

This provides further opportunity for students to discuss their work situations and how complaints are dealt with. You could ask students to work in groups of four. After discussion, two students in the group act out the dialogue and the other two are observers who can comment on how the complaint is handled. They then change roles. Remind students about the six steps for dealing with complaints that they worked on earlier in the unit and tell them that you want to hear authentic intonation in both roles. Go around the class, monitoring and supporting. Ask some students to perform their dialogues in front of the class.

More words to use

Write these words on the board: *dirty, uneatable, stained, short-staffed, blocked, dripping, undercooked, cracked, frozen, torn*. Tell students to look up any new words in the Glossary. Ask students to read the words aloud and check pronunciation.

16 Mistakes and problems

⁘ **Situations/functions**
Checking details
Finding a solution
Offering compensation

⁘ **Structures**
Indirect questions

■ Revision of Unit 15

Expressions to learn

Tell students that you are a hotel guest making complaints. Give them the complaint scenarios from the unit and get responses from around the class. Elicit the expressions for sympathizing with a customer, reassuring them and promising action to put things right.

New words to use / More words to use

Make flashcards of the words (see Unit 2). Always include any new words that students have contributed in stories about their work experience.

Other revision suggestions

- Practise the Present Perfect by asking questions about what students have(n't) done/seen/finished, already/yet/just/today. Also ask questions with *How long ...?* to elicit sentences using *for* and *since*.
- Get students to practise dialogues in groups of three, reading the first Listening script from Unit 15.
- Tell students to do the Activity from Unit 15, working with a different partner.

■ Starter

Introduce the topic of mistakes. Mistakes are made, even in the best of hotels and restaurants. (If you want to lighten the topic, try and get hold of one of the BBC TV *Fawlty Towers* DVDs – hilarious episodes of Basil Fawlty and his wife running a hotel and restaurant in the UK available worldwide). Look at the pictures together, one by one, and ask students to contribute to tell the story. Keep it light – don't insist on correct grammar, just get their contributions about what they can see (the pictures depict the scenario in the first Listening). Ask if students have got any stories of mistakes made where they have worked. How were they dealt with? Was any compensation offered?

■ Listening *Sorry, it's our mistake*

Pre-teach unfamiliar vocabulary from New words to use (see Introduction).

1 🎧 16.1 Give students a minute to look at the exercise. Review any vocabulary as necessary. Play the recording and ask students to tick the correct information. Check answers around the class.

Answers

1 wrong rooms
2 rooms not adjoining
3 no disabled facilities
4 no sea view
5 wrong name keyed in by reception
6 move guests out of wrong rooms
7 transfer Johnsons' luggage into right rooms
8 free meal in the restaurant

2 🎧 16.1 Tell students to read sentences 1–8. Stronger students may be able to complete them without listening again. Play the recording again and ask students to complete/check the sentences. Check answers around the class. Point out the use of the passive in number 7 – hotel policy is not to blame colleagues in front of guests.

Answers

1	mistake with	5	so sorry
2	explain	6	sorted, out
3	adjoining, disabled facilities	7	when you
4	take a seat	8	accept

Practise the Expressions to learn before doing exercise 3.

3 Ask students to use the prompt steps to practise the situation in Listening. Alternatively, they can use a situation from their own experience or the following.

- table booked for special occasion for ten / no record of booking / only remaining table on bar terrace / customer doesn't want this / offer complimentary bottle of champagne in bar while they wait 30 minutes for another table

■ Language study

Expressions to learn

Ask students to read the expressions aloud. Check pronunciation and intonation. Ask students to learn the expressions for homework.

New words to use

Elicit the words from around the class by giving students prompts (see Unit 1). Check pronunciation of any difficult words and get students to repeat after you. Ask students to learn the new words for homework.

Language check

Indirect questions

Illustrate the difference between direct and indirect questions by writing two contrasting sentences on the board: *What's your name?* (spoken in a sharp monotone) *Could you tell me your name?* (spoken with rising and falling intonation). Ask students how they would prefer to be spoken to if they were a customer. Stress how important it is to begin conversations with indirect questions to avoid appearing rude, especially in customer service situations. In natural English conversation, we mix indirect questions with direct questions.

Read the notes and examples with the class. Point out: the change in position of the verb (it moves to the end of the sentence); the auxiliary verb *do* isn't used in indirect questions; how *if* or *whether* are used when there is no question word in the direct form. Ask students to read the phrases around the class once or twice, practising intonation. Tell students to refer to the notes and use a variety of the phrases in bold to change the questions into the indirect form. Check answers around the class.

Model answers

1 Do you know where the nearest post office is?
2 Could you tell me what your name is?
3 Could you let me know how many nights you're staying?
4 Do you know if the tour rep comes to the hotel ...?
5 Could you tell me if you checked the time ...?
6 Could you let me know what time you'd like lunch?
7 Do you remember where you last saw your passport?
8 Do you know what you're going to do today?
9 Do you remember your tour rep's name?
10 Do you know if you want dinner tonight?

■ Listening *I'm sure we can sort something out*

1 🎧 **16.2** Play the recording and elicit the two problem situations. For lower-level students, play the recording again. Ask students to note down the two staff actions in each dialogue. Check answers around the class.

Answers

1 The woman's flight has been cancelled.
The group's table isn't ready.
2 The receptionist offers to check accommodation availability and suggests the woman emails her office. The waitress brings menus into the bar for the group and serves them a complimentary champagne cocktail.

Ask students if they or their colleagues have ever had to deal with similar problem situations. How did they handle them?

2 🎧 **16.2** Ask students to match the parts of the sentences. Play the recording again to check answers. Tell them to listen carefully to the receptionist's and waitress's intonation. Ask them to read the sentences aloud around the class.

Answers

1 i   2 h   3 a   4 b   5 e   6 c   7 f   8 d
9 j   10 g

3 Give a few prompts on the board for the customer role: 1 *flight cancelled – no flights for two days – due back at work – nowhere to stay*; 2 *table not ready – booked 8.30 – want to eat soon*. Ask students to take turns as customer and staff and use the language in exercise 2 to deal with the problems.

■ Activity

Allow plenty of time for students to study their roles, check the language they are going to use in the dialogues and even practise with their partner before putting the whole scenario together. In this activity, you could give half the class the reception role-play and the other half the restaurant scenario. Divide the class into pairs, Student A and Student B, and direct them to their roles. Give them time to read their information and ask any questions. Encourage students to stand up and improvise a reception desk and restaurant reception. Go around the class, monitoring and supporting. Ask some students to perform their dialogues in front of the class.

■ More words to use

Write these words on the board: *blind, deaf, lame, guide dog, walking stick, wheelchair, crutches, hearing aid*. Tell students to look up any new words in the Glossary. Ask students to read the words aloud and check pronunciation.

Giving advice and assistance

⟳ **Situations/functions**
Helping with lost luggage and lost passports
Emergencies and first aid

⟳ **Structures**
First and second conditionals

■ Revision of Unit 16

Expressions to learn

Remind students about dealing with mistakes and people's problems as politely as possible. Elicit expressions for: apologizing for mistakes, checking what's wrong, sympathizing with a customer's situation, offering a solution, offering compensation. Pretend you're a customer with a problem and give individual students sentences to respond to: *I've got the wrong room. / My flight's been cancelled. / We booked a table by the window. / I booked a room fitted for disability. / We asked for a room with a balcony.*

New words to use / More words to use

Make flashcards of the words (see Unit 2). Include any new words that students have contributed in stories about their work experience.

Other revision suggestions

- Give students direct questions (use the list in the Language check) and ask them to form indirect questions. If necessary, let them read the Language check notes first and then tell them to close their books.
- Get students to practise dialogues in pairs, reading one of the dialogues in the Listening script from Unit 16.
- Tell students to do the Activity from Unit 16, working with a different partner.

■ Starter

Travellers often arrive at reception with some kind of problem. Ask students what they think the most common problems are. Tell students to look at the pictures and identify what items they think the guests are missing. Don't give the answers at this point (**a** luggage **b** passport) as they will find out when they hear the situations in the Listening. Ask students how they would deal with guests with lost or stolen property. What advice would they give? Find out what situations they or their colleagues have experienced on reception. What advice was given?

■ Listening *Lost property*

Pre-teach unfamiliar vocabulary from New words to use (see Introduction). Half of the words are from the second Listening, which deals with an emergency. Identify any first aiders in the class who can help you later in the unit.

1 ⊙ **17.1** Give students a minute to read the questions. Play the recording and ask them to answer the questions. Check answers around the class.

Answers

> 1 Her luggage is lost.
> 2 Contact the airport for an update.
> 3 Freshen up before the welcome meeting (when the tour rep will advise her what to do).
> 4 His passport.
> 5 Maybe it's on the coach or fell out of his rucksack.
> 6 He left it on the bank counter.

2 ⊙ **17.1** Tell students to read sentences 1–6 and complete any they can. Play the recording again and ask students to complete/check the sentences. Ask students to read their answers aloud as you check them around the class.

Answers

1 labelled	3 freshen up	5 fell out of
2 local store	4 everywhere	6 best thing

Practise the Expressions to learn before doing exercise 3.

3 Ask students to use the expressions, exercise 2 and the prompts to practise the situations from the Listening. Make sure they take turns to be guest and receptionist. You could pair weaker (guest) and stronger (receptionist) students for the first run through of the dialogues as the guest only needs to make minimal responses (e.g. *Yes/No, Thank you*).

■ Language study

Expressions to learn

Ask students to read the expressions aloud. Check pronunciation and intonation. Ask students to learn the expressions for homework.

New words to use

Elicit the words from around the class by giving students prompts (see Unit 1). Check pronunciation of any difficult words and get students to repeat after you individually and chorally. Ask students to learn the new words for homework.

Language check

First and second conditionals

Stronger students will already have mastered the conditionals, so move quickly on to the exercises. With a mixed-level class, elicit when we use the first conditional (for very likely or possible situations). Read the examples. Point out the alternative ways of saying the sentences (with *if* + condition either in the first or second part of the sentence) and the sequences of the present and future tenses. Elicit when to use the second conditional (for unlikely or unreal situations). Ask what tenses are used (Past simple and *would* + verb). Read the examples and point out the alternative position of *if* + condition again. Highlight how *unless* can replace *if … not* in conditional sentences. Elicit more examples using *unless*, e.g. *I won't book a table unless you call me.* Grammatically speaking, the verb *be* in the second conditional is *were* for all persons. But in modern usage, most native speakers say: *If he/she/it was … .* However, the phrase *If I were you … , I would …* is still commonly used for giving advice.

1 Remind students about the sequence of tenses and ask them to underline the correct alternative. Correct answers around the class.

Answers

1 will	3 will	5 will
2 would contact	4 had	6 would

2 Tell students they have four things to think about in this exercise: whether the condition is likely or unlikely, the tenses used, their sequence and their position according to where *if/unless* is in the sentence. Look at the examples together and then ask them to complete the sentences. Tell them to compare with a partner before checking answers around the class.

Answers

3 won't call, have	6 went, would visit
4 spoke, would ask	7 close, will fall out
5 won't contact, finds	8 wouldn't know, stole

■ Listening *Can you call a doctor?*

1 Give students who are interested in first aid an opportunity to show their knowledge. It could be fun to get them to demonstrate the relevant vocabulary in New words (and other procedures they know) on volunteer patients!

2 🎧 **17.2** Ask students to read the first-aid procedures in the box. Play the recording and ask them to tick the procedures carried out. Ask them to compare with a partner and then check answers around the class.

Answers

call ambulance, calm and reassure patient, lie patient flat, loosen clothing, put in recovery position, raise legs

3 🎧 **17.2** Play the recording again and ask students to number the sentences in the correct order. Lower-level students may like to listen again. Check answers around the class.

Answers

a 2 b 4 c 5 d 9 e 1 f 7 g 6 h 3 i 8

4 With lower-level students, you could let them read the Listening script and listen again before they write their dialogues. Make sure they practise their own dialogue and not just read the script from the book. Go around the class, helping and supporting. Check that the students in David's role sound suitably calming and reassuring.

■ Activity

This is a fun end-of-unit activity, which practises the second conditional form. Ask students to work with a partner. Give them a few minutes to read the list of situations and query any vocabulary. While they do the activity, go around the class, monitoring and giving vocabulary support where necessary. Get early finishers to think up their own situations and continue working with a partner. Name students around the class to ask the questions to students other than their partner.

■ More words to use

Write these words on the board: *choke, clinic, strain, plaster, unconscious, nosebleed, fracture, dislocation, bandage, burn, convulsion, bleeding, pulse, wound, sprain.* Tell students to look up any new words in the Glossary. Ask students to read the words aloud and check pronunciation.

:→ **Situations/functions**
Difficult phone calls
Clarifying, checking, repeating and spelling

:→ **Structures**
The Passive

■ Revision of Unit 17

Expressions to learn

Elicit expressions for giving advice/help to guests with problems. Give situations to respond to: *I've lost my passport. / The airline's lost our luggage. / We've missed our plane.* You could write prompts on the board to elicit specific expressions: *contact airport/update, don't shop unless urgent, airport find luggage/send to hotel, checked belongings?, ask tour rep/she'll advise, I call airport?, if/spoke the language/call them, when/last see?*

New words to use / More words to use

Make flashcards of the words (see Unit 2).

Other revision suggestions

- Practise first and second conditionals around the class. Give students the first part of a sentence to complete with a suitable phrase in the right tense.
- Get students to practise dialogues in pairs, reading one of the dialogues in the Listening script from Unit 17.
- Tell students to do the Activity from Unit 17, working with a different partner.

■ Starter

Ask if any students have attended a telephone-training course. Were they told to actively smile into the phone when talking to customers? They are usually advised to do this. Customer care on the phone is very important in most businesses. Tell students to read the list of possible difficulties when communicating in English on the phone. Some students may tick all the boxes, which would be perfectly normal. Find out if anyone has experiences they feel comfortable talking about. Elicit what they would say if: the phone line is bad; someone is speaking very quietly or too fast; they don't understand people's names. Ask if anyone is familiar with any of the international telephone alphabets to help with spelling (the most popular one is on page 101 of the Student's Book).

■ Listening *A difficult call*

Pre-teach unfamiliar vocabulary from New words to use (see Introduction). Most of the words are in the context of phone calls.

1 ⌒ **18.1** Tell students they are going to hear a receptionist coping with a difficult call. Play the recording and ask them to mark the difficulties both the receptionist and the caller had. Check answers around the class.

Possible answers

> a bad line, difficult to catch name (maybe different accents), receptionist spoke too fast for caller, caller possibly spoke quietly, English was probably a foreign language for both caller and reception

2 ⌒ **18.1** Tell students to read the extracts and complete any they can. Play the recording again and ask students to complete/check the extracts. Ask students to read the mini-dialogues aloud around the class.

Answers

> 1 bad line, you repeat
> 2 Is that F, It's S for
> 3 was, was logged
> 4 after eleven, catch
> 5 give me, faint, speak up

3 Ask students to work with a partner and make notes for a phone call dialogue, following the steps in the flow chart. Tell them to refer to the language in the expressions and exercise 2. Give them five minutes to prepare, and then ask them to sit back to back to practise the call. Make sure they change roles. Go around the class, monitoring and supporting.

■ Language study

Expressions to learn

Ask students to read the expressions aloud. Check pronunciation and intonation. Ask students to learn the expressions for homework.

New words to use

Elicit the words from around the class by giving students prompts (see Unit 1). Check pronunciation of any difficult words and get students to repeat after you. Ask students to learn the new words for homework.

Language check

The Passive

Ask students to read the notes and examples. If students are unsure of how to form the Passive, refer them to the Language review on page 92. Elicit examples of when it's sensible to use *by* in a Passive sentence and when to leave it out. Point out that the Passive is a useful structure for working people. Working in shifts and in a team, we can't be personally responsible for all customer service. It allows us to distance ourselves from procedures, e.g. *the call was logged, their rooms have been held*. We don't have to use *I* or *we* or involve a colleague who is not present. Ask students to read the example sentences and then to complete the exercise, only using *by* where appropriate. Check answers around the class.

Answers

3 Kraus is spelt with an S not an F.
4 The adjoining rooms were held for Mr Kraus.
5 Parking spaces are normally booked in advance.
6 The ferry has been delayed by bad weather.
7 The call was logged at 6 p.m.
8 The car is being delivered in half an hour.
9 Directions are going to be sent (by the receptionist) in an email attachment.
10 A car park exit code will be provided at check-in.

■ Listening *Communication on the move*

Use the picture at the bottom of the page to elicit possible problems when communicating by mobile phone rather than a landline. This will review any new words students haven't used yet: *no signal, weak signal, signal breaking up, getting cut off*. Review how we write/talk about email addresses: *upper case/capitals, lower case, @ (at), . (dot), .com, no space, all one word, hyphen, underscore, attach, forward, pdf, jpg*.

1 🎧 18.2 Tell students they are going to hear a phone conversation between a customer on a train and Karin, an events organizer at the Hotel Bristol. Tell them to look at the information they need in order to complete Karin's notes. Play the recording (twice if necessary). Ask students to compare with a partner before checking answers around the class.

Answers

1 Dekko	5 Tuesday, 5th December
2 PRL	6 cristinadekko@prl.es
3 product launch	7 pdf of events brochure
4 300	

2 🎧 18.2 Tell students to read the questions. Play the recording again and ask students to note the answers. Check answers orally around the class.

Answers

1 She's returning Mrs Dekko's call.
2 She's on a train and the signal isn't very good.
3 Call back on a landline as soon as she can.
4 Information about hiring the venue.
5 By email.
6 The signal breaks up/They get cut off.

3 You could set this for homework if you are short of class time. If necessary, refer students back to Unit 5, which focused on writing skills.

Model email

Thank you for your enquiry about holding your product launch at the Hotel Bristol. I confirm that our conference suite is available on Tuesday, 5 December. We will be very happy to organize an event for around 300 delegates.

We attach a copy of our events brochure for your information.
We look forward to hearing from you.
Best regards

■ Activity

Ask students to read through Expressions to learn again. Do a quick revision of days and dates and tell students to have the international alphabet at the back of their books ready to refer to. Divide the class into pairs, Student A and Student B, and direct them to their roles. Give them time to read their information and ask any questions. Tell students to sit back to back and begin the calls. If feasible, you could get students to use their own mobiles. Ask some students to perform their dialogues in front of the class.

■ More words to use

Write these words on the board: *extension, coverage, crackling, interference, cell phone, satellite phone, handset, receiver, engaged, beep, dial tone, charger, text message*. Tell students to look up any new words in the Glossary. Ask students to read the words aloud and check pronunciation.

19 Conference and meeting enquiries

⇛ **Situations / functions**
Talking about facilities and services
Explaining conference packages

⇛ **Structures**
Managing a conversation

■ Revision of Unit 18

Expressions to learn

Elicit the expressions by giving individual students situations to respond to: *You didn't catch their name. / Their voice is very faint. / They are speaking too quickly/ quietly. / The line is bad. / Ask them to repeat dates. / Thank them for calling to tell you. / Reassure them their rooms are being held. / Query how to spell something.* Alternatively, use the flow chart on page 38.

New words to use / More words to use

Make flashcards of the words (see Unit 2).

Other revision suggestions

- Have a list of ten short sentences ready that will sound natural in the Passive (with one or two where *by* would be used). Give one example and then drill the sentences around the class a few times by asking students to change the sentence into the Passive. Example sentences: *The receptionist logged the call earlier. / Bad weather delayed the flight (by). / The receptionist sent the email yesterday. / The noise in room 305 kept the guests awake all night (by). / Reception will give the guests a car park permit when they check in. / The hotel held the rooms for the late arrivals. / You spell Dekko, D-E-K ... .*
- Get students to practise dialogues in pairs, reading one of the dialogues in the Listening script from Unit 18.
- Tell students to do one of the Activity role-plays from Unit 18, working with a different partner.

■ Starter

There is a lot of quite difficult vocabulary in this unit relating to conference services and facilities. Even if students have met some of it before in *Highly Recommended* 1, spend some time reviewing the language by talking about the items in the pictures. Ask students to read the list of facilities. Help with unfamiliar vocabulary. Ask students which facilities they think are essential and why. Golf course and

swimming pool are the only non-essentials. Car parking in a nearby public car park could also be an option.

■ Listening *A tour of the conference suite*

Pre-teach unfamiliar vocabulary from New words to use (see Introduction). Give the context students will meet in the listening. Encourage them to learn the words in phrases (collocations): *seating capacity, seats 40 comfortably, room layout, multimedia equipment, plenary session, purpose-built centre, various sizes/ options.*

1 🎧 **19.1** Tell students they are going to hear a customer being given a tour of a conference suite. Give them a few minutes to read the information they have to complete. Play the recording (twice if necessary). Tell students to compare with a partner and then check answers around the class.

Answers

1 nine	4 classroom	6 partitioning
2 30	5 15	7 50
3 U-shaped		

2 🎧 **19.1** Read the words in the box aloud and ask students to repeat. Tell them to read sentences 1–8 and complete any they can. Play the recording again and ask students to complete/check the sentences. Ask students to read answers aloud as you check them around the class.

Answers

1 purpose-built	4 capacity	7 breakout
2 delegates	5 comfortably	8 sliding doors
3 plenary	6 programme	

Practise the Expressions to learn before doing exercise 3.

3 Ask students to work with a partner and use the language in the expressions and exercise 2 to talk about the rooms and equipment in the pictures. They can make up the seating capacity of the rooms and add any other facilities and equipment. The customer can ask questions about seating capacity, the different room layouts and the equipment available. Make sure they change roles. Go around the class, monitoring and supporting.

Alternatively, you could ask students to talk about the room they are in. They could make a sales presentation of the room as a meeting room and include extra facilities/equipment.

■ Language study

Expressions to learn

Ask students to read the expressions aloud. Check pronunciation and intonation. Ask students to learn the expressions for homework.

New words to use

Elicit the words from around the class by giving students prompts (see Unit 1). Ask students to look again at the pictures and elicit the names of the facilities and equipment. Write a list on the board. Check pronunciation of any difficult words and get students to repeat after you. Ask students to learn the new words for homework.

Language check
Managing conversation

Ask students to think about their own language and the little words (with no real meaning) that they use to start a conversation, change a topic, get someone's attention or emphasize a point. Give a little ten-second 'speech' yourself with some examples of these conversation markers. It is these words and hesitations that make our spoken language sound natural rather than like a formal presentation. Also ask students about the sounds and words we use to show that we are listening to someone (active listening). Ask students to read the notes and examples in their books. Tell students to turn to the Listening script on page 78 and first underline all the conversation markers and then find the woman's active listening responses. Get them to read the script aloud in pairs.

■ Listening *Planning an event*

Tell students that the Listening is a phone call from a customer enquiring about organizing a training seminar at a hotel. Ask students what information they would ask for if they were the customer. Review vocabulary from New words to use that wasn't used in the first Listening.

1 🎧 **19.2** Tell students to look at the information about The Meeting Place. Play the recording and ask them to complete the information. Tell them to compare with a partner and then check answers around the class.

Answers

1 multimedia	5 wireless broadband	8 sit-down
2 breakout	6 €66	9 Residential
3 whiteboards	7 buffet	10 €180
4 flipcharts		

To consolidate the difficult vocabulary in this unit, you could play the recording again and ask questions around the class: *What is Bob Delaney planning in June? What's the seating capacity of the main lecture hall? How many breakout rooms are there? What equipment is in the breakout rooms? What Internet facility is there? What's included in a day delegate package? How much is that? What additional services are in the residential package?*

2 Ask students to work in pairs as customer and conference organizer. They can use the information about The Meeting Place or adapt it with their own ideas. Go around the class, monitoring and supporting. You could give lower-level students the opportunity to look at the Listening script before doing this exercise.

■ Activity

Tell students that this consists of one phone call and one face-to-face meeting. Ideally, you want everyone to experience both the A and B roles, so try and leave plenty of time for this activity. Divide the class into initial pairs, Student A and Student B, and direct them to their roles. Give them time to read their information and ask any questions. Stress the importance of active listening for both scenarios – on the phone the speaker might think they've been cut off unless they hear some encouraging noises! Also tell them to remember to use markers to signal change of topic or emphasize a point. *Right* or *Well* can also give thinking time while they are working out what to say next. Tell students to sit back to back for the first dialogue. Go around the class, monitoring and supporting. Ask some students to perform their dialogues in front of the class.

■ More words to use

Write these words on the board: *AV equipment, handout, interactive whiteboard, auditorium, microphone, rostrum, schedule, state of the art, wall-mounted, spacious*. Tell students to look up any new words in the Glossary. Ask students to read the words aloud and check pronunciation.

20 Handling payments

⋯▷ **Situations/functions**
Dealing with guests' bills
Payment security

⋯▷ **Structures**
Revision of numbers

■ Revision of Unit 19

It may be best to revise the vocabulary first as there were probably a lot of difficult and unfamiliar words.

New words to use / More words to use

Make flashcards of the words including all the names of pieces of equipment recycled in the Starter (see Unit 2). Write phrases on some cards to encourage the use of collocations (*plenary session*, *seating capacity*, etc.).

Expressions to learn

Ask students questions about the conference centre plan on page 41 to elicit the expressions and vocabulary.

Other revision suggestions

- Elicit how to show that you're listening actively to someone (*Right, Good, OK, I see, Mmm, Ah*). Ask for words used to manage a conversation when starting to explain something (*Well, So*), changing the topic (*Now*), emphasizing a point (*Actually*).
- Get students to practise dialogues in pairs, reading one of the dialogues in the Listening script from Unit 19.
- Tell students to do one of the Activity role-plays from Unit 19, working with a different partner.

■ Starter

There is often confusion about the different types of cards used for payments. The main types in international use are:

credit card (e.g. Visa, Mastercard) – customers can use this to buy goods and services and pay for them later; they are billed six-weekly for what they have spent – interest is charged on outstanding balances.

debit card – a personal bank card (e.g. Lloyds) which allows customers to take money directly from their bank when they pay for something (these cards may also be marked Visa).

charge card (e.g. American Express/AMEX) – customers pay an annual fee for this card, which works the same as a credit card but the monthly bill has to be paid in full.

Tell students to look at the picture of different payment methods and identify them around the class. Ask which ones they are familiar with. Have they taken payments (or made them) using cards or traveller's cheques? Can they explain the procedures?

■ Listening *Settling hotel bills*

Pre-teach unfamiliar vocabulary from New words to use (see Introduction). Give students the context they will meet in the Listening. This would be a good time to talk about currencies and exchange rates relevant to your students. Get them to check the exchange rates of their currency with the US dollar and euro or with another currency used in their country.

1 🎧 **20.1** Tell students they are going to hear two customers settling their bills. With a mixed-level class, you could play the dialogues one at a time and check students' understanding. Ask students to read the questions first and then play the recording. Tell them to compare answers with a partner before checking answers around the class.

Answers

> 1 No. They're complimentary.
> 2 The amount for phone calls.
> 3 Yes.
> 4 His company is invoiced for the room and breakfasts. He pays for the extras in cash.
> 5 A single room supplement.
> 6 Dinner and one night's accommodation.
> 7 Mastercard.
> 8 The Mastercard receipt and the hotel receipt.

2 🎧 **20.1** Ask students to read the sentences and match them to make mini-dialogues. Play the recording again to check answers.

Answers

> 1 c 2 f 3 e 4 g 5 d 6 a 7 b

Practise the Expressions to learn before doing exercise 3.

3 Ask students to look at the incomplete bill printout and work with a partner to complete the prices and total in their local currency. Then ask them to use the receptionist and guest prompts to talk about the bill and make payment. With stronger students, the guest could make up their own queries about the bill for the receptionist to respond to.

■ Language study

Expressions to learn

Ask students to read the expressions aloud, completing any unfinished sentences with their own phrases. Check pronunciation and intonation. Ask students to learn the expressions for homework.

New words to use

Elicit the words from around the class by giving students prompts (see Unit 1). Check pronunciation of any difficult words and get students to repeat after you individually and chorally. Ask students to learn the new words for homework.

Language check
Revision of numbers

Read through the table with the class, dealing with any queries. Note that *zero* is frequently used instead of *oh*, e.g. €420 = *four-two-zero euros*. Get students to give you amounts in money and exchange rates that they are familiar with and write them on the board. To practise students' competence in speaking numbers, prepare flashcards for an oral test. Write different numbers on small cards and keep them for repeated use, e.g. *496*, *Room 372*, *$87.46*, etc. Hold up a flashcard and ask individual students to call out the answer. You could add a competitive element by awarding points for correct answers. Get students to correct any wrong answers.

■ Listening *Payment security*

Ask students what problems there might be with customers' payments at checkout, e.g. bank note forgeries. Ask students with work experience if they have examples to tell the class.

1 🎧 20.2 Play the recording and ask students to note the list of problems that occur when taking payments. Check answers around the class.

Answers

> 1 forgeries of large notes
> 2 queries of bill items
> 3 stolen cards
> 4 invalid cards (out of date/date expired)
> 5 signatures don't match
> 6 stolen cheques

2 🎧 20.2 Ask students to read the five situations and check understanding. Play the recording again and tell students to note down what advice is given. Tell students to compare with a partner before checking answers around the class.

Answers

> 1 Inform the manager in the back office.
> 2 Check the bill carefully; if customer is wrong, take them into office to explain.
> 3 Take a swipe of the card and reassure customer that no payment is taken (it's just for security purposes).
> 4 Ask for expiry date and starting date (if there is one), the 3-digit security number on the back of the card and the long number on the front.
> 5 Ask customer to sign (countersign) the cheques in front of you; compare the signatures with signature in customer's passport.

3 Tell students to work with a partner and use the answers from the previous two exercises to ask each other for advice for the situations in exercise 2, e.g. A: *What shall I do if a banknote looks like a forgery?* B: *Take it to the manager in the back office.* Write some prompts on the board to help: *What shall I ask for when taking …? What shall I check when taking/accepting …?*

■ Activity

Divide the class into pairs, Student A and Student B, and direct them to their roles and the relevant bills. Give them time to read their information and ask any questions. To make the activity more realistic, you could ask students to write out (or word process) the bills on pieces of paper so they can present them to the guest checking out. Alternatively, ask students to make up their own bills. Remind students that they can use the language from Expressions to learn and exercise 2 from the first Listening. Student A starts the first dialogue: *I'd like to settle my bill.* Go around the class, monitoring and supporting. Ask some students to perform their dialogues in front of the class.

■ More words to use

Write these currencies on the board: *peso, krona, franc, bolivar, dinar, dong, new lira, koruna, pound, rupee, rial, kuna, zloty, dirhan, dollar.* Ask students if they know where any of the currencies are used. Tell them to check on page 100 of the Student's Book. Ask students to read the words aloud and check pronunciation.

21 Explaining and training

⇢ **Situations/functions**
Kitchen hygiene and safety
Following instructions
Cooking processes

⇢ **Structures**
Obligation and prohibition

■ Revision of Unit 20

Expressions to learn

Tell students you are a guest checking out of a hotel. Give them the first line of a typical receptionist/guest dialogue for this situation. If necessary, give them a prompt for the response (see brackets): *Could I settle my bill, please? Room 451* (printout). / *I don't think the amount for phone calls is right* (itemized list). / *You've overcharged me by one night* (our mistake). / *I'll pay by Visa* (card in machine, enter PIN, remove card).

New words to use

Make flashcards of the words including the different types of payment recycled in the Starter (see Unit 2). Write phrases on some cards to encourage the use of collocations (*company account, itemized bill,* etc.).

Other revision suggestions

- Recycle some of the number flashcards used in the unit and ask students to say the numbers.
- Get students to practise dialogues in pairs, reading the first Listening script from Unit 20.
- Tell students to do one of the Activity role-plays from Unit 20, working with a different partner.

■ Starter

This will be revision for students who have already done training in hygiene and safety. Put students in small groups and ask them to make a list of possible rules. Tell them to look at the picture for ideas first and then close their books (in case some students look below and just copy the guidelines in exercise 2). All students should make a copy of the list as it's needed for the next exercise. Compare and discuss lists around the class. Use the picture to help with vocabulary.

■ Listening *Kitchen rules and regulations*

Pre-teach unfamiliar vocabulary from New words to use that is going to come up in the first Listening (see Introduction). Leave the cooking terms for now (*glaze, overlapping, prick, roll out, roughly, stiff, trim*).

1 🎧 **21.1** Tell students they are going to hear the first part of a training session between a chef and three students (those in the picture). The session is about kitchen hygiene and safety. Play the recording and tell students to tick any rules on their lists that they hear and to make a note of those not on their lists. See exercise 2 for model answers. Answers in note form are fine, e.g. *always wear cap.*

2 🎧 **21.1** Ask students to read the jumbled sentences and try to put the words in the right order. The first word of each sentence has initial capitals to help them. The guidelines are in the same order as in the Listening. Play the recording again with pauses to check answers.

Answers

> 1 Please make sure you always wear clean, hygienic clothing.
> 2 Wearing a cap in the kitchen is compulsory.
> 3 You'll have to tie your hair back.
> 4 At the end of each shift all work surfaces have to be scrubbed and cleaned.
> 5 I'm sorry, but you can't wear them (earrings) in the kitchen.
> 6 It's important to report all illnesses and infections to Chef.
> 7 You mustn't use the slicer without the guard in place.
> 8 We have to keep all the raw, cooked and fresh foods separate.

Practise the Expressions to learn before doing exercise 3.

3 Ask students to work in pairs. For the first few minutes, allow them to use the answers for the previous exercise and the expressions to respond to the prompts. Then ask them to cover both these and continue responding. If students ask for explanation of the key structures at this point, jump ahead to the Language check and then come back to the exercise. Go around the class, monitoring and supporting. Don't worry if the answers are not in exactly the same words as the Listening script as long as students are using the relevant vocabulary.

Language study

Expressions to learn

Ask students to read the expressions aloud. Check pronunciation and intonation. Ask students to learn the expressions for homework.

New words to use

Elicit the hygiene and safety words from around the class by giving students prompts (see Unit 1). The second Listening continues the training session with food preparation instructions. Use the context of the listening to help explain the words. Ask if any students are familiar with pastry-making – they may enjoy demonstrating the different processes. Check pronunciation of any difficult words and get students to repeat after you individually and chorally. Ask students to learn the new words for homework.

Language check

Obligation and prohibition

Keep this simple. *Must* and *have to* are almost identical in their use. Just tell students that when they're reminding themselves about an obligation, they use *must*: *I must phone my mum. I must get some cash from the bank. I must do some revision tonight.* Read the notes with the class – use the Language review on page 94 for extra information. Point out that interestingly, the opposite sense of *must* is *needn't* rather than *mustn't*. *Mustn't* is used in a different context, forbidding or prohibiting you from doing something – it could be stopping you from doing something dangerous: *You mustn't touch the hot ovens without protection.* Ask students to read the sentences in the exercise and underline the correct alternative. Check answers around the class.

Answers

1 must	4 must	7 have to
2 don't have to	5 mustn't	8 mustn't
3 needn't	6 can't	

■ Listening *Following a recipe*

Recap on the cooking words in New words before you start.

1 🎧 21.2 Tell students to read stages a–j. Play the recording and ask students to put the instructions in the right order. Play the recording again with pauses to check answers.

Answers

a 2	b 7	c 10	d 8	e 3	f 6	g 1	h 5		
i 9	j 4								

2 🎧 21.2 Ask students to read the verbs in the box and try to complete the phrases with them. Make sure that nobody is copying from the script at this stage. Tell them to compare answers with a partner. Play the recording again for them to complete or correct their answers. Check answers around the class.

Answers

1 sift	5 melt	9 trim
2 rub in	6 simmer	10 bake
3 mix	7 puree	11 heat
4 peel, core	8 slice	12 brush

3 Divide the class into groups of four – one person for each of the flan-making stages. Tell students to turn to the Listening script on page 80 and make notes about their stage in the preparation of the flan. Then ask them to take turns to give instructions to the group for their stage of the recipe. Write some sequence markers on the board for them to use: *first, next, then, after that, finally.* Go around the class, monitoring and supporting the groups.

■ Activity

Tell students that they're going to practise giving both food hygiene and safety rules and cooking instructions. Divide the class into pairs, Student A and Student B, and direct them to their roles and the recipes on page 66. Give them time to read their information and ask any questions. Check any unknown vocabulary in the recipes. Encourage stronger students to write their own recipes. Tell weaker students to recap by looking back at the Expressions to learn and exercise 2 in the first Listening. Point out that in each scenario the chef will give some kitchen rules and the trainee will ask questions about other rules, which the chef must answer. Go around the class, monitoring and supporting. Ask some students to perform their dialogues in front of the class.

■ More words to use

Write these words on the board: *roll, soak, blanch, squeeze, blend, shred, discard, sprinkle, moisten.* Tell students to look up any new words in the Glossary. Ask students to read the words aloud and check pronunciation.

22 Working in housekeeping

‹›› **Situations/functions**
Servicing a room
The evening turndown service

‹›› **Structures**
have something done

■ Revision of Unit 21

Expressions to learn

Ask students why kitchen hygiene and safety rules are so important (they help to stop the spread of infection and food contamination). Elicit all the kitchen hygiene and safety rules they can remember (there are 11 altogether in exercise 2 and the expressions). Give prompts to keep things moving as in exercise 3 on page 44.

New words to use / More words to use

Make flashcards of the words including the cooking and food preparation terms in exercise 2 on page 45 (see Unit 2). If students get a cooking term flashcard, they have to give you a sentence to show its use, e.g. *prick – Prick the base of the pastry case with a fork.*

Other revision suggestions

- Write *must, have to, don't have to, needn't, mustn't, can't* on the board. Elicit sentences relating to hygiene and food safety rules and regulations.
- Tell students to do one of the Activity role-plays from Unit 21, working with a different recipe and a different partner.

■ Starter

Ask students, in turn, to call out the items they can see on the trolley in the picture. List the items on the board under shelves (e.g. *Top shelf*). Check that everybody agrees with the name of an item and understands what it is – some are very easy and obvious, others more difficult. Elicit any other items that might be on a room attendant's trolley.

Answers

Top shelf: body lotion, shampoo, shower gel, soap, shower hats, shoe shine cloths, glasses
Middle shelf: sheets, pillow slips (pillow cases), towels, bathmat
Bottom shelf: toilet rolls, box of cleaning products, cloths, black rubbish bags, stick duster
Side: bin, soiled laundry bag

■ Listening *Servicing a room*

The Starter will have revised/taught a lot of the vocabulary in the Listening. Pre-teach any remaining unfamiliar vocabulary from New words to use (see Introduction). All the words are in the first Listening apart from *fluff up (the pillows)*. Ask if any students have experience of room servicing or elicit the procedures they've learnt in their training.

1 🎧 **22.1** Ask students to look at the Order of work chart and check they understand the tasks. Clarify that item k refers to faults or damage in a room; item m – reporting high-value guest items left behind – would be done immediately the items are found; item p refers to damaged linen. Play the recording and ask students to work in pairs to number the tasks in the order they hear them. It's quite a long recording, so you may need to play it with pauses for lower-level students. Play the recording again with pauses and check answers around the class.

Answers

a 7	b 9	c 16	d 5	e 10	f 13	g 1	h 15
i 2	j 8	k 14	l 12	m 3	n 11	o 4	p 6

Hotels may train their staff to work in a different order. Ask students about their experience and discuss in class if relevant.

2 🎧 **22.2** Ask students to read sentences 1–8 and complete them where they can. Play the recording again for them to check/complete their answers. Check answers around the class.

Answers

1 put, keep	5 there's
2 around, under	6 throw away
3 Fold, with the pillows	7 have to
4 Tie, linen	8 stain, gone

Practise the Expressions to learn before doing exercise 3.

3 Tell students that the sentences in exercise 2 and the expressions will help them explain the tasks. Encourage students to make the trainee role more than active listening by asking questions like: *Where shall I put the soiled linen/dirty towels? What shall I do with the bedspread? Shall I throw these away? Shall I check the drawers? Shall I mop the floor now?* Write some of these on the board. You could introduce a bit of action by

getting students to move around and mime the tasks. Go around the class, monitoring and supporting.

Language study

Expressions to learn

Ask students to read the expressions aloud. Check pronunciation and intonation. Ask students to learn the expressions for homework.

New words to use

Elicit the words from around the class by giving students prompts (see Unit 1). Check pronunciation of any difficult words and get students to repeat after you individually and chorally. Ask students to learn the new words for homework.

Language check

have something done

Get students to personalize this by putting across the idea of paying for somebody to carry out an expert service for them: they have their hair cut, their teeth treated, their pets looked after while they are on holiday, etc. Read the notes with the class. Point out the form of the different tenses. Read the prompts and the example in the exercise and ask students to make sentences with the correct form of *have something done*. Check answers around the class.

Answers

> 1 The hotel had the first floor refurbished last year.
> 2 Mr Banks is having his hair cut in the hotel salon later today.
> 3 The housekeeper hasn't had the carpets cleaned for several months.
> 4 The conference office is having its multimedia equipment updated next month.
> 5 Chef always has fresh salmon delivered from Scotland.
> 6 Have you had the fire alarms tested recently?
> 7 We have the air conditioning serviced twice a year.
> 8 The manager had new hotel stationery printed last month.

This unit is also a good opportunity for a recap on things that *need doing* (Unit 14). You could make questions from some of the situations above for students to respond to, e.g. *Does the first floor need refurbishing? – No, it doesn't need refurbishing. They had it refurbished last year.*

Listening *Providing added value*

Ask students if they are familiar with the nightly 'turndown service' that many hotels offer. Exactly what is done varies from hotel to hotel. Ask students about any experience they have of this service.

1 🎧 22.2 Tell students to read the list of Turndown service instructions at the top of the page. The Listening is about the turndown service in two guest suites. Tell students to listen and mark the tasks in the list *S2* or *S3* accordingly. Play the recording. Check answers around the class.

Answers

> S2 – remove bedspread, fluff up pillows, turn bed down, place chocolate and card on pillow, close curtains
> S3 – everything except replenish supplies and toiletries, clean toilet and polish mirror

2 Divide the class into groups for discussion. Ask students to focus on questions 1 and 2. When they've finished, ask a member of each group to report back on the thoughts of the group.

Activity

Tell students they're going to practise explaining the tasks involved in servicing a room and in a turndown service. Divide the class into pairs, Student A and Student B, and direct them to their roles and the relevant pictures. Explain that both students look at the picture on page 47 when Student A is the experienced room attendant and the picture on page 65 when Student B is in this role. Give students time to read their information and ask any questions. Encourage students in the trainee role to participate as much as possible by asking questions. Go around the class, monitoring and supporting. Ask some students to perform their dialogues in front of the class.

More words to use

Write these words on the board: *shower cap, shoe shine cloth, pen, pencil, Do Not Disturb notice, duvet cover, bath mat, sewing kit, notepaper, bathrobe, envelope.* Tell students to look up any new words in the Glossary. Ask students to read the words aloud and check pronunciation.

23 Health, safety and security

⟶ **Situations/functions**
Health, safety and emergency procedures
Security issues
⟶ **Structures**
should/shouldn't, ought to

■ Revision of Unit 22

Expressions to learn

Brainstorm room-servicing procedures around the class. Give prompts if necessary. Then do the same with the turndown service.

New words to use / More words to use

Make flashcards of the words, including any vocabulary items on the room attendant's trolley which caused difficulty (see Unit 2).

Other revision suggestions

- Elicit examples of services/jobs that hotels, schools and colleges have done, how frequently they have them done, and when they last had them done (imaginary time scales are fine, but try to get students to use different tenses).
- Ask students to do one of the Activity role-plays from Unit 22, working with a different partner.

■ Starter

Look at the signs in the picture together and work out what they mean and where they might be seen (fire extinguisher, caution wet floor, drinking water, hazard, toxic hazard, CCTV camera, first aid, electric shock risk, no admittance). Write any new vocabulary on the board. Ask students if they know any similar signs (maybe in kitchens and staff areas where they work or study). Remind students about the kitchen hygiene and food safety situations they met in Unit 21 and recap on the relevant vocabulary.

■ Listening *Minimizing risks*

The Starter should have provided a good introduction to this relatively long listening with its specialist vocabulary. Continue by pre-teaching unfamiliar vocabulary from New words to use (see Introduction). Remember that the words are best remembered when they are in context and often a phrase is easier to remember than a single word.

1　🎧 **23.1** Ask students to look at the words in the box and check they understand the meaning. With stronger students, ask them to work in pairs to try and complete the sentences. Then play the recording to check or complete the exercise. Alternatively, play the recording for students to complete the sentences as they listen. Check answers around the class. Ask if anybody is familiar with the saying *You don't have to be a rocket scientist*? (You don't have to be super intelligent – it's basic knowledge.)

Answers

1 germs and bacteria	4 slip	7 unattended
2 toxic	5 trip	8 security
3 Worn	6 fire alarm	

2　🎧 **23.1** Tell students to read the parts of the sentences and check they understand the vocabulary. Ask them to try and match the sentence parts before they listen again to the recording. Play the recording and ask students to check/complete their answers. Check answers around the class.

Answers

1 e	2 h	3 g	4 b	5 c	6 d	7 a	8 f

Practise the Expressions to learn before doing exercise 3.

3　Tell students that the sentences in exercises 1 and 2 and the expressions will help them with their discussion. Encourage students to include different or additional procedures from their own experience. Draw the activity to a close by asking for contributions on the discussion items from all members of the class.

■ Language study

Expressions to learn

Ask students to read the expressions aloud, completing the two unfinished expressions with their own phrases. Check pronunciation and intonation. Ask students to learn the expressions for homework.

New words to use

Elicit the words from around the class by giving students prompts (see Unit 1). Check pronunciation of any difficult words and get students to repeat after you individually and chorally. Ask students to learn the new words for homework.

Language check

should, ought to

Ask students to read the notes and examples. Point out that *Ought you?* (question form) and *oughtn't* (negative) exist but aren't often used.

1 Tell students to look carefully at the phrases in the box and use each of them once in the correct form.

Answers

1 shouldn't use	5 ought to tell
2 ought to report	6 should call
3 shouldn't leave	7 shouldn't come
4 should you put up	8 should guests do

2 You may like to substitute topics more relevant to the students' environment here. Ask students for ideas of situations where they would give strangers or tourists advice on what they *should* or *shouldn't do* in a country.

■ Listening *Key words: health, safety and security*

1 ⌒ **23.2** Ask students to read the key words and check they understand them all. Play the recording and ask students to number the key words in the order they hear them. Check answers around the class.

Answers

1 warning sign	7 assembly point
2 infestation	8 fire extinguisher
3 suffocation	9 emergency procedures
4 unauthorized personnel	10 bacteria
5 bomb threat	11 evacuation
6 roll call	12 fire drill

2 The Challenge game is particularly aimed at students who find the specialist vocabulary challenging. Warn students that they have three minutes to complete the table while you read the definitions. Use the definitions in the Listening script on page 82 but say them in this order: suffocation, bacteria, emergency procedures, infestation, warning sign, fire drill, evacuation, unauthorized personnel, assembly point, bomb threat, fire extinguisher, roll call.

Answers

infestation, fire drill/extinguisher, assembly point, emergency procedures, bacteria, unauthorized personnel, fire extinguisher/drill, suffocation, bomb threat, warning sign, roll call, evacuation

An alternative activity, to lighten up a serious subject, is a variation on charades. Students work in groups of four. One member of Group A acts out a key word or phrase for the group to guess while Group B watches. If Group A guesses correctly, they get 1 point. Then the 'actor' has to give the correct definition (another 1 point). If they can't guess after one minute, Group B has a chance to give the answer and score 1 point and a further 2 points for the correct definition.

■ Activity

Tell students they are going to do a quiz on the topic of the unit. You could organize it in small groups. Students make a note of the answers and then you check them orally around the class giving each group an opportunity to answer in turn. Alternatively, divide the class into two teams with you as the quizmaster. The quizmaster asks individuals in each team a question (alternating the teams). If the individual answers correctly, the team scores 2 points. If they can't answer, the individual's team can try for 1 point. If still no correct answer, the opposing team can try for 1 point. Maximum score is 22 points. Anything over 17 is very good.

Suggested answers

1 a) Inform chef/person in charge of health and safety.
  b) Lock it away in the right place/Give it to your supervisor.
  c) Inform security.
  d) Take a fire extinguisher and put it out.
2 Tell them to leave their room immediately and come to the assembly point.
3 You would leave the building and close all doors and windows behind you to stop the fire spreading.
4 Take a roll call of guests and staff to see if anyone is missing.
5 You should wear rubber gloves when handling kitchen waste.
6 To evacuate the building is the most important thing.
7 To minimize the risk of germs/bacteria spreading.
8 Never put yourself at risk. An intruder could be violent.

■ More words to use

Write these words on the board: *explosion, tornado, firearms, flood, sensor, inspection, poisonous, identity badge, hurricane.* Tell students to look up any new words in the Glossary. Ask students to read the words aloud and check pronunciation.

Countries and cultures

⇢ **Situations/functions**
Making plans
Talking about different customs

⇢ **Structures**
Verb + -*ing* or (*to*) infinitive

■ Revision of Unit 23

Expressions to learn

Elicit the expressions by giving prompts (e.g. *toxic cleaning products, wet floor, unattended package, stranger in the building, you feel unwell one morning*) or asking questions about health, safety and security: *What does a member of staff do when there's a fire they can't control? What should guests do when they hear the fire alarm?*

New words to use / More words to use

Make flashcards of the words (see Unit 2).

Other revision suggestion

• Ask students to work in pairs to ask and answer the Activity quiz questions.

■ Starter

1 Ask if any students have travelled abroad alone and been through airports. Then ask students to match the airport places with the activities. Check answers around the class.

Answers

> 1 b 2 d 3 a 4 c

2 Divide the class into small groups and ask them to discuss what other things happen at the four airport places. Procedures vary from country to country and from year to year. Students may have interesting stories about their experiences of going through passport control or security. Ask groups to report back to the class.

Possible answers

> 1 check tickets and passports, label and hand over luggage, information on departure times, boarding times and gate numbers
> 2 last-minute seat allocation, pushchairs, wheelchairs, etc. handed over to airline staff
> 3 X-ray screening of hand luggage, body searches, removal of any liquids of more than 100 ml
> 4 check of visas as well as other immigration papers

■ Listening *Work experience abroad*

Ask if any students are planning to go on work placements abroad. Give them a little time to talk about their travel plans. Tell students that the Listening is a discussion between two young people who are going abroad and the airport procedures one of them goes through. Pre-teach unfamiliar vocabulary from New words to use (see Introduction).

1 🎧 24.1 Ask students to read the sentences for Part A. Play the recording and ask them to underline the correct alternative. Repeat for Part B. Check answers around the class.

Answers

> 1 to work   7 the departure gate number
> 2 won't have much   8 in the tray
> 3 English   9 wanted to search him
> 4 Emil   10 scanned
> 5 three   11 has
> 6 may be a problem   12 the hotel

2 🎧 24.1 Play the recording again and ask students to complete the sentences. Check answers around the class.

Answers

> 1 some time   4 unattended   7 mobile behind
> 2 to climb   5 Keep checking   8 provides us
> 3 filled in, off 6 through

3 Tell students to study the first five Expressions to learn, which are useful for discussing travel plans. Ask them to think about where they'd like to work abroad. Then divide the class into small groups and tell them to come to a unanimous decision about where they would all like to go. They must be able to give reasons and justify their decision. Ask a spokesperson from each group to explain their choice to the rest of the class.

As an extra activity, ask students to work with a partner from another group and take turns to be passenger and official. The passenger is travelling to the destination chosen above and goes through check-in, security and arrivals. Write prompts on the board:

Passenger

Decide: how many bags you have, including hand luggage; where you want to sit; which metal objects you have in your pocket; how long you're staying in the country; where you'll live.

Official

You are the check-in official, the security official and the passport officer at arrivals.

Tell the 'official' to use the Listening script on page 82 to talk to the passenger.

■ Language study

Expressions to learn

Ask students to read the expressions aloud, completing the unfinished expressions with their own phrases. Check pronunciation and intonation. Ask students to learn the expressions for homework.

New words to use

Elicit the words from around the class by giving students prompts (see Unit 1). Check pronunciation of any difficult words and get students to repeat after you. Ask students to learn the new words for homework.

Language check

Verb + *-ing* or (*to*) infinitive

Remind students of the verb patterns from Unit 12 (recommending, suggesting and advising). Ask students to read the notes and examples, and use the Language review on page 94 for extra information. Tell students to complete the exercise. Check answers around the class.

Answers

1	to visit	4	to lock	7	to get
2	working	5	to help ... find	8	leave
3	sitting	6	writing		

■ Listening *Festivals around the world*

1 Tell students to read the names of the six festivals. Ask if they know or can guess where and when the festivals are celebrated. Ask if they can tell you what language the names are in. Can they guess the possible content of the festivals?

2 Divide the class into pairs, Student A and Student B, and direct them to their reading texts. Tell students that you want them to do a quick 20-second scanning exercise. The only information you want them to look for is the place and time of each festival. After 20 seconds, get them to share the information with their partner. Check answers.

Answers

Santa Lucia: Sweden, 13th December; Carnival: around the world (Brazil is mentioned), February/March before Lent; Loy Krathong: Thailand, full moon of the 12th month (November in West); Hanami: Japan, end March to beginning of May; Carnival of Viareggio: Italy, January–February; Up Helly Ae: Shetland, last Tuesday of January

3 Give students five minutes to read the texts more carefully.

4 Ask students to answer the questions and then compare and discuss their answers with their partner. Tell them not to read each other's texts. Check answers orally around the class.

Answers

1 Santa Lucia (Christian), Carnival (Roman Catholic), Loy Krathong (Buddhist)
2 Santa Lucia (candles), Hanami (lanterns), Loy Krathong (candles)
3 Carnival Viareggio (floats, performers, music), Up Helly Ae (marching, dancing)
4 Santa Lucia (white clothes, candles), Hanami (quiet thinking), Loy Krathong (floating rafts)
5 Santa Lucia, Hanami, Up Helly Ae
6 Carnival of Viareggio (We don't know when the festival of Up Helly Ae began.)

■ Activity

Tell students that they are going to prepare some information about a festival. Students can work in pairs or small groups. They can research information as a homework task and then pool information in the lesson to prepare their presentation. As a variation, you could ask students to prepare a poster to describe their festival. They could illustrate it with pictures and write some details about the festival. They could then display their poster on a board or table and be ready to describe the festival. Presentations could be given in small groups rather than to the whole class. Alternatively, if presentation work isn't suitable for your class, you could set this as a written composition task.

■ More words to use

Write these words on the board: *lantern, raft, blossom, dishes, costume, dancing, mask, musicians.* Tell students to look up any new words in the Glossary. Ask students to read the words aloud and check pronunciation.

Situations/functions
Differences between cultures
Advising on cultural norms

Structures
Reporting verbs

■ Revision of Unit 24

Expressions to learn

Elicit the expressions by asking students to give sentences useful for discussing travel plans. Give prompts: *I plan to … / I'd love to … / I'm looking forward to … / I've decided to … / I managed to …* . Ask what questions are often asked about luggage at an airport check-in.

New words to use / More words to use

Make flashcards of the words (see Unit 2).

Other revision suggestions

* Write some pairs of verbs on the board: *enjoy/travel, finish/work, promise/give, remember/call, keep/try, let us/leave, enjoy/meet*, etc. Ask students around the class to choose one pair and give a sentence using the verbs. Remind them that the second verb will be the *-ing* form or the infinitive with or without *to*.
* Ask students to work in pairs and discuss the festival they researched or one of the festivals from the Reading.

■ Starter

Ask students what they understand by the word *culture* when talking about a country or a region. Encourage their contributions and make a list on the board: *art, literature, music, language, dress, customs, traditions, religion, attitudes, history, geography, climate, archaeology, natural resources, industries*. Ask students to contribute typical characteristics of their own cultures – everything that makes their country or region what it is today. Ask what they think about any stereotypical ideas that foreigners may have about their country. Encourage students to be sensitive about other cultures and not to sum them up in stereotypes – this could be offensive. Introduce the idea that companies like hotel groups have a culture: the image they want people to have of them, management style, organization, training and development opportunities, etc. Ask students to work in pairs or small groups to talk about how people greet each other in their culture and other cultures that they know. Ask pairs/groups to report back to the class.

■ Listening *Unexpected experiences*

Ask if any students have travelled abroad. Were there any surprises which they realized were due to their new experience of a different culture? Pre-teach unfamiliar vocabulary from New words to use (see Introduction). To *save face* is to stop someone being embarrassed. To allow someone to *lose face* in Chinese culture is an insult.

1 🎧 **25.1** Tell students they are going to hear five guests talking about their experiences in foreign hotels. Play the first extract and ask if students agree with the example answer given. Play the recording, pausing after each extract for students to note down what the guest was surprised about. Play any extracts again if requested.

Answers

> 2 The food was good but the restaurant was empty.
> 3 The waiter didn't clear the plates when they'd finished eating.
> 4 The receptionist didn't give eye contact and was shocked when the guest put his business card on the desk.
> 5 The receptionist told them not to drop litter, chew gum or tip staff.

2 Divide the class into small groups and tell them to discuss the five experiences and try to think of an explanation for each. After a few minutes, elicit suggestions and move on to exercise 3, which will give the explanations.

3 Tell students to read the notes a–e and match each one with a situation in exercise 1.

Answers

> a 4   b 2   c 1   d 5   e 3

■ Language study

Expressions to learn

Ask students to read the expressions aloud, completing the unfinished expressions using the notes in exercise 3 or their own phrases. Check pronunciation and intonation. Ask students to learn the expressions for homework.

New words to use

Elicit the words from around the class by giving students prompts (see Unit 1). Check pronunciation of any difficult words and get students to repeat after you individually and chorally. Ask students to learn the new words for homework.

Language check

Reporting verbs

Introduce the topic of reported speech – reporting back on what someone has said. Give a few examples using *say/tell*:

'The lesson finishes at four o'clock'. The teacher said the lesson finishes at four o'clock.
'Open your books'. She told us to open our books.

Tell students that several other verbs can be used to report what people say. When the guests were reporting their experiences in the Listening, they used *apologize, blame, assure, offer, warn, advise, refuse* and *ask*. For example, in the first extract the woman would have said something like: *I'm sorry for making a mess*. Reported back this becomes: *I apologized for making a mess*.

1 🎧 **25.1** Ask students to look at sentences 1–6. Play extracts 1, 3 and 5 again, and ask students to listen for the reporting verb used in each sentence. Check answers around the class.

Answers

1 apologized	4 warned
2 blamed	5 advised
3 assured, offered	6 refused, asked

Read the notes about the different patterns that can follow reporting verbs. Ask students to look at the sentences in exercise 1 and underline the reporting phrases, e.g. *apologized for making*.

2 Tell students to read the example and then complete the exercise, referring to the pattern rules above. Check answers around the class. You could use exercise 4 in Test yourself 5 (page 95) or exercise 3 on page 52 of the Workbook to consolidate the use of the reporting verbs.

Answers

2 advised her to call
3 assured me that
4 offered to take us
5 warned them not to drop
6 refused to accept

■ Listening *Cultural differences*

Write *What makes cultures different?* on the board. Brainstorm a list of ideas with the class. Tell students they're going to hear two people discussing this topic.

1 🎧 **25.2** Ask students to read the sentences. Play the recording and ask them to mark *true* or *false* as they listen. Check answers around the class.

Answers

1 false	3 true	5 false	7 true
2 true	4 false	6 false	8 true

Ask students if they have experienced any of the issues in the Listening in their own work/life. Are there similar issues in their own culture that might affect travellers?

2 Divide the class into small groups and ask them to discuss the questions. Ask a spokesperson from each group to present their ideas to the class.

■ Activity

Tell students they are going to compile some information/advice for someone coming to live or work in a different culture. Read through the activity with the students and check that they understand all the vocabulary. Ask students to work in pairs. Give each pair a sheet of flipchart paper (have some Blu-Tack available) and ask them to make notes, using some of the ideas listed or adding their own. When they've finished, divide the class into groups of six and get each pair to present their ideas, using their notes. Go around the class, monitoring and supporting. Encourage students to make any changes to their information after they've listened to each other's presentations.

■ More words to use

See Workbook page 53 for a vocabulary extension exercise based on a reading text.

Working life

■ Revision of Unit 25

Expressions to learn

Ask students to turn to the expressions on page 52 and number them 1–7. Ask students to complete them with their own phrases as you drill them around the class.

New words to use

Make flashcards of the words (see Unit 2). Include any words from the Listenings and the Activity which were new to students.

Other revision suggestions

- Elicit reporting verbs that can be used instead of *say* and *tell* and write them on the board. Make pronouncements and ask students to report your words. Point to a verb on the board for each pronouncement, e.g. *I'm really sorry about the mistake.* (apologize) *He/She apologized for the mistake. Don't look at the answers.* (warn) *He/She warned us not to look at the answers.*
- Ask students to work with a partner (from a different group to their group in the Activity) and discuss the information they compiled.

■ Starter

Tell students to look at the pictures. Elicit what jobs the people do and what tasks they are likely to do at work. Ask students what they think are the most enjoyable parts of each job (e.g. chef: working with food, creating dishes, working in a team, having responsibility; receptionist: meeting people, practising foreign languages, helping people, working in a team, working in a pleasant environment; room attendant: working with other people, varied tasks). Then ask students what they think are the least enjoyable parts of the jobs, e.g. working in heat and under pressure, dealing with rude people, long hours, working shifts, working weekends, sometimes having to do unpleasant tasks. Ask students which of the jobs they would most like to do and why.

■ Listening *About my job*

1 🎧 **26.1** Tell students to study the information before you play the recording, so they know what they need to listen for. Play the recording and ask students to complete the information. Play section by section with pauses for lower-level students. Ask students to compare answers with a partner and then check answers around the class.

Answers

1 two months	7 encouraging
2 meeting people	8 have own restaurant
3 pay	9 nearly a year
4 work most weekends	10 working with fun team
5 work in South America	11 strict
6 learning from boss	

You could ask students who are working to do a similar profile for their jobs and to compare workplaces with a partner doing a similar job.

2 🎧 **26.1** Ask students to read sentences 1–6 and try to correct them. Play the recording again for students to check their answers.

Answers

1 I enjoy most	3 with	5 improve
2 checking in	4 alternate	6 about

Draw students' attention to the phrase *I'm busy checking in*, which is difficult to translate in many languages. *To check in* is a main verb; it doesn't need *make* or *do* to turn it into an action word as in *make an arrangement, do the staff rota*. After *busy*, use the *-ing* form of the verb, e.g. *busy dealing with guests, busy answering the phone.* There are several examples of idioms in the Listening which you could exploit with your fast finishers or stronger students. Write the following sentences from the Listening on the board and elicit or teach the meaning of the idioms in bold.

1 *We often meet up when we're **off duty**.* (not at work)
2 *He'll **have a laugh** with us when reception is quiet.* (enjoy a joke)
3 *I'd been **out of work** for three weeks.* (unemployed)
4 *I was **over the moon** when I got this job.* (very happy)
5 *I was called in **at short notice** to work extra shifts.* (with very little warning)
6 *He was always putting me **on the spot**.* (in an awkward situation)

7 *He says I have **the makings of** a fine chef.* (the potential to be)

8 *Making beds might not be **everyone's cup of tea**.* (what everyone likes to do)

9 *We're all **on the same wavelength**.* (all think the same way)

3 Tell students to work with a partner and use the information in exercise 1 to ask and answer questions about the three people.

4 Ask students to ask and answer questions about their own jobs or work experience. Encourage them to move around the class, talking to different people to find out their stories of working life.

Language study

Expressions to learn

Ask students to read the expressions aloud, completing the unfinished expressions with their own phrases. Check pronunciation and intonation. Ask students to learn the expressions for homework.

New words to use

Elicit the words from around the class by giving students prompts (see Unit 1). Check pronunciation of any difficult words and get students to repeat after you. Ask students to learn the new words for homework.

Language check

Adjective + preposition

Tell students that even advanced students of English find it difficult to get adjective + preposition structures right. If they can learn these 18 common adjective + preposition phrases, it will be a good start! Give students a few minutes to study the list of examples. Tell them to read the example sentences and emphasize that the phrases can be followed by a noun/pronoun or a verb in the *-ing* form. Ask if students can clarify the difference in meaning between: *good for* (a benefit) and *good at* (expert); *responsible for* (in charge of) and *responsible to* (she's my boss). Ask them to do the exercise. Check answers around the class.

Answers

1 suitable for	6 good for
2 interested in	7 responsible to
3 good at, good at	8 excited about
4 proud of	9 aware of
5 famous for	10 responsible for

■ Listening *The story of success*

Most students should have heard of Jamie Oliver (young English chef famous for his informality as well as his cooking). If anybody hasn't heard of him, elicit information from the more knowledgeable students. You could ask students to check the Internet or their library resources before or after the lesson for more information.

1 🎧 26.2 Tell students to read sentences 1–10, and check any vocabulary they're not sure of. Play the recording and ask students to underline the correct alternative. Check answers around the class.

Answers

1 London	6 spending a lot of money
2 head pastry chef	7 travels a lot for his work
3 dropouts	8 more expensive
4 a great success	9 healthy
5 junk food	10 the US

2 Students may already have someone in mind that they would like to research. If not, help with suggestions. Give guidance as to where students can find out information: on the Internet, the college or public library, specialist magazines. This may have to be a project for a later lesson. If you have a large class, divide it into groups of four to six students and ask students to present their information to the group in turn. Go around the class, monitoring and supporting.

■ Activity

1 Ask students to think of their dream job in the hospitality industry. Then tell them to work with a partner and try to guess each other's dream job. The person being questioned can only answer *Yes* or *No*. After ten questions, the questioner must try and guess what the job is. They can ask another ten questions if necessary but if they still haven't discovered what the job is, they have to give up.

2 Tell students to continue by asking each other what they might like and dislike about their dream jobs. Refer them to Expressions to learn for help with the language.

■ More words to use

Look at the list of personnel on page 101 of the Student's Book. Tell students to look up any new words in the Glossary. Ask students to read the words aloud and check pronunciation.

⇢ **Situations/functions**
Personal qualities, skills and experience
CVs and covering letters
⇢ **Structures**
Talking about the future
Question tags

■ Revision of Unit 26

Expressions to learn

Ask students questions to elicit the expressions (they may need to refer to the expressions first, but then get them to close their books): *What do you think of your new job? / What do you enjoy most about it? / Is there anything you don't enjoy? / How do the shifts work? / How long have you worked on reception? / How long have you been here? / What were you frightened of? / What's your goal?* Go around the class until they can answer fluently.

New words to use

Make flashcards of the words (see Unit 2).

Other revision suggestions

- Give individual students an adjective and ask them to make a phrase, e.g. *pleased – pleased with me / in charge – in charge of making bread / responsible – responsible to the housekeeper.*

- Ask students to work in pairs and discuss what they would most like and least enjoy about their chosen dream jobs.

■ Starter

Your students may be just thinking about their first job application, or they may be seasoned applicants already working in the hospitality industry. Writing a CV was covered in *Highly Recommended* 1, but updating or improving a CV is a useful exercise. Pick and choose whatever is relevant for your students from this unit. It may be most useful for your class at the beginning of the college year.

There is a lot of specialist vocabulary in the unit so the Starter is a good place to begin with all students. Don't rush this part of the unit. The language will be useful for a lifetime of job applications, covering letters and interviews. First model the pronunciation of the words and phrases. Read them aloud and ask students to repeat after you. Divide the class into pairs and give them ten minutes to check the meaning of the words

and phrases. If any are causing particular difficulty, clarify them for the whole class. Ask students to choose five of the words or phrases to best describe themselves and five to describe their partner. Then ask them to compare and discuss with their partner.

■ Listening *What are my strengths?*

Explain the meaning of *strengths*. Ask around the class for examples of their partner's strengths. Tell students to ask a partner about their special interests. Ask for some examples around the class. Help with vocabulary and write a list of contributions on the board for later use.

1 🎧 **27.1** Tell students they are going to listen to three students talking about applying for jobs. Play the recording (twice if necessary) and ask students to note each person's strengths and special interests. Check answers around the class. Note that the word *stuff* is common in its colloquial use when the speaker doesn't want to sound too organized or detailed in their explanation, e.g. *A: What did you talk about? B: Oh, you know. Stuff. A: What did you do last night? B: Oh, just listen to music and stuff.*

Answers

Eva:	leadership skills, good team worker, first aid
Chris:	good communication skills, leadership skills
Sophie:	hard-working, reliable, good team worker, confident, well organized, conscientious

Practise the Expressions to learn before doing exercise 2.

2 Ask students to work with a different partner to brainstorm the items listed (all this information is needed for a CV and/or covering letter). Tell them to ask and answer questions, and suggest ideas for each other. They should make a note of all the information about themselves. Go around the class, monitoring and supporting.

Note that this activity would make an excellent practice opportunity for question tags (see Language check). You could jump forwards to this section and then return to exercise 2, telling students to practise question tags in the brainstorming with their partner.

3 If you would like your students to work on their CVs, tell them to turn to page 67 and study the *Writing your CV* tips. Give them a copy of the photocopiable

CV template on page 63 of this book. You may need to key in or enlarge this. Or if you have the facilities, ask students to open a personal folder on their PCs for all their job application information and key it in themselves. It is generally accepted that a CV is typed, but employers often prefer application forms and covering letters to be handwritten. If this is obligatory, it is usually stated in the job advert.

■ Language study

Expressions to learn

Ask students to read the expressions aloud. If you have already reviewed question tags, ask students to tag a question onto the expressions where appropriate, e.g. *Joanne's really good at writing, isn't she?* Check pronunciation and intonation. Ask students to learn the expressions for homework.

New words to use

Elicit the words from around the class by giving students prompts (see Unit 1). Check pronunciation of any difficult words and get students to repeat after you. Ask students to learn the new words for homework.

Language check

Talking about the future: *going to* and *will*
Remind students about the Present Continuous for future plans or arrangements, which was covered in Unit 4 (e.g. *We are refurbishing the guest rooms on the first floor later this year*). Read through the notes and examples with the class. Make sure they know the difference between: a planned intention (*going to*) and a last-minute decision (*will*); a prediction based on knowledge or evidence (*going to*) and one based on hope, thoughts or luck (*will*).

1 Ask students to decide which category of the future (*P, I* or *D*) the sentences fall into. Check answers around the class and discuss any confusion.

Answers

1 I	2 D	3 P	4 P	5 D	6 I	7 P	8 P

Question tags

Read the examples carefully with the class. Point out how the main verb and tag verb are in the same tense. Highlight the sequence of negative verb followed by positive tag and vice versa.

2 Ask students to complete the exercise. Tell them to compare answers with a partner and then check answers around the class.

Answers

1 won't you?	5 has she?
2 hasn't he?	6 aren't you?
3 were you?	7 did he?
4 didn't you?	8 can you?

■ Writing *Covering letters*

Ask individual students to read the Covering letter tips one by one. Check meaning. Use the board to illustrate letter layout: position of company address (top left), own address (top right), date (under own address). Ask students to look at the jumbled letter and work with a partner to put the parts of the letter in the best order. Then ask individual students to come to the board and write each section of the letter (or at least the first four or five words of each section). Ask students to copy the corrected letter to keep for reference as a model.

Answers

a 8	b 7	c 5	d 4	e 3	f 9	g 6	h 2
i 10	j 12	k 11	l 1				

■ Activity

Tell students they are going to practise writing a covering letter. This could be started in class and completed at home. Suggest that students find a partner they can work with at home or can communicate with by email. Go through the instructions with the class and check they understand what to do. Tell them to look on the Internet or in their local press to see the form of an advertisement (or you could direct them to the Unit 28 adverts on page 67 as reference). Encourage students to get all the advice they can from their partner (and their family/friends if appropriate). Tell them that their final draft covering letter can be word processed.

■ More words to use

Write these words on the board: *date of birth, bonus, surname, desirable, probation, temporary, permanent, essential, ideal candidate*. Tell students to look up any new words in the Glossary. Ask students to read the words aloud and check pronunciation.

Job interviews

⇢ **Situations/functions**
Interview questions and answers
Interview tips

⇢ **Structures**
Past Simple or Present Perfect?

■ Revision of Unit 27

Expressions to learn

Elicit the expressions by asking students to tell the class some of the qualities of their partner or another person they know.

New words to use / More words to use

Make flashcards of the words (see Unit 2). Include phrases from the list of qualities in the Starter.

Other revision suggestions

- Remind students about the use of *going to* and *will*. Tell them to ask a partner: what they're going to do when they leave college, where they hope to live, what they think their exam results will be, when they're going to start applying for jobs, what they're going to say about themselves in covering letters, when they think they'll start work.
- Ask students to work in pairs and make a list of eight tips for writing covering letters.

■ Starter

Tell students to look at the pictures. Explain that the young man has a job interview. Establish what the man is doing wrong in each picture and ask what advice students would give him for his next interview. Help with vocabulary and introduce relevant words from New words to use.

Suggested answers

a He should take more care with his appearance (neat clothes and clean shoes); he should leave more time to get ready and travel to the interview so that he's not rushed and sweating.
b He should sit comfortably in the chair not slouched; he should look interested and enthusiastic.
c He should try and relax and not look so nervous; he should look at the interviewer when he's speaking (and talk clearly).

Ask if any students have attended interviews. Did they feel they presented themselves well? Were there any ways that they felt unprepared? Has the experience taught them anything useful that they can use next time?

■ Listening *Interview questions and answers*

1 🎧 **28.1** Tell students to read questions 1 and 2 before you play the recording. Play the recording and give students a few minutes to discuss the questions with a partner before checking answers.

Suggested answers

1 Osman was the better candidate: confident and enthusiastic, good communication skills, relevant experience, good attitude, good answers to questions, ambitious. Selma lacked confidence and she also seemed unenthusiastic and unprepared for the interview, and had no relevant experience.
2 Can you tell me a little bit about yourself? Why do you want this job? Do you enjoy working with other people? What sort of job would you like in five years' time? Are there any questions you'd like to ask me?

2 🎧 **28.1** Play the recording again and ask students to complete the sentences.

Answers

1 worked for	5 let me know
2 do something, uses	6 for, on reception
3 listen to, enjoy, shopping	7 work hard
4 ago	8 Is there

3 Emphasize how important it is to prepare for interviews. Read the exercise instructions with the class and check they understand what they have to do. Ask them to study the Expressions to learn. Tell them to think of a job they'd like for the question: *Why do you want this job?* Ask them to sit facing each other as interviewer and interviewee when they are asking and answering questions. Insist that all students spend a few minutes thinking about question 2. Compare suggestions around the class. Advise students to avoid asking questions about pay, holidays, days off, and details like travel to work, lunch breaks, sick pay and work contract details. Enquiries about training, career opportunities, starting date, information about the company, opportunity to use languages would all show interest and enthusiasm for the post.

Language study

Expressions to learn

Tell students that this is a list of typical interview questions. To practise pronunciation and intonation for the Activity, ask students to read the expressions aloud.

New words to use

Teach the remaining unfamiliar words in the context of the Interview tips in the Reading. Check pronunciation of any difficult words and get students to repeat after you. Ask students to learn the new words for homework.

Language check

Past Simple or Present Perfect?

Both of these should be familiar to students. However, it is useful for students of all levels to review and compare the use of the tenses. Ask students to read the notes and examples. Complete the exercise around the class.

Answers

```
 1  started, 've just finished
 2  hasn't applied, left
 3  's had, hasn't had
 4  went, didn't have
 5  Have you heard, called, didn't get
 6  was offered, hasn't accepted
 7  Have you ever worked, 've only worked
 8  left, was born, 've lived
 9  Have you ever applied, I've never applied
10  have you been, did you do
```

Reading *Interview tips*

1   Ask students what things they would think about if they were invited for a job interview. Elicit contributions that cover the criteria in a–d. Draw students' attention to these four categories. Ask them to read the Interview tips and put each tip in the correct category. Tell them to compare with a partner and then check answers around the class. Note that enthusiasm and smile (9) could be c or d.

Suggested answers

a 1, 4, 12	c 5, 6
b 2, 8, 10, 11	d 3, 7, 9

2   Divide the class into groups of four and ask them to discuss the questions. Go around the class, monitoring and supporting. Ask different students in each group for feedback on the questions.

Activity

This should be good fun as well as useful. Set the tone of the activity by stressing that interviewers need to be positive and constructive, and sensitive to the interviewee. The aim of the activity is to practise answering interview questions and to help build confidence for 'the real thing'. In some cultures interviews may be handled differently or students may not be used to hearing comments about themselves, in which case adapt the activity (i.e. end the activity after students have interviewed each other). However, students who intend to work in an international environment, may have to undergo a similar, standard interview procedure and they need to be prepared for this. For the group part of the activity (3), take care how you assign students to groups in a mixed-level class (mix stronger with weaker students).

1   Direct students to the job ads. Ask them to choose one and study it.

2   Tell students to work with a partner and practise asking and answering interview questions, using the Expressions to learn.

3   Divide the class into groups of four. If you think your students can cope with it, give them 12 (three each) copies of the Assessment sheet (see page 63 of this book). Their first task is to note the name of the interviewee on the sheet and the job he or she has chosen. They should use the sheet to assess the person's different qualities and to make any other notes. Before each interview, students will need to decide who will ask which questions. They may need to adapt their questions according to the chosen job. Each interview should last ten minutes.

When the four interviews have been completed, ask the groups if they would like to discuss the Assessment sheets together and give constructive feedback to the interviewee. Close the session with general feedback from the groups about the experience: what they liked/disliked about it, what they learnt from it, what they need to work on to improve their interview techniques.

More words to use

Write these words on the board: *intelligent*, *sullen*, *poised*, *amenable*, *engaging*, *anxious*, *assertive*, *sophisticated*, *cooperative*, *emotional*, *sympathetic*, *aggressive*. Tell students to look up any new words in the Glossary. Ask students to read the words aloud and check pronunciation.

Model answers

Unit 5, Writing, exercise 4

Subject: For your information
Dear Mr Lomo

Thank you for your email.
We are pleased to confirm your reservation for 3 nights from Tuesday 4 to Friday 7 December.

Best regards

Unit 5, Language check, exercise 2

Dear Mr Wollmann

Thank you for your recent letter.
We enclose a copy of our brochure as requested.
We look forward to seeing you next week.

Yours sincerely

Unit 5, Listening, exercise 2

1 Dear Mrs Pele
Regarding your booking enquiry, we are pleased to confirm your reservation of an ensuite twin room for three nights from 6 January.

2 Dear Mr Feinds
Regarding your recent request to change the details of your booking, we are pleased to confirm that we are now holding three double and three single rooms for seven nights from 10 May.
We look forward to seeing you then.

3 Dear Ms Kowlski
We confirm your booking of a double room for five nights from 12 February.

4 Dear Ms Lee
I'm afraid that the restaurant is fully booked for lunch on 13 July.
We would be happy to arrange a table for you in the Terrace Bar with the restaurant menu.

5 Dear Mr Fox
Thank you very much for your message enquiring about our wedding services.
We are pleased to confirm that we have a party room available on 25 June next year.
We enclose our Special Events brochure and some buffet and sit-down meal menus for your information.
We hope we can be of service to you.

Unit 5, Activity

Email
From: reservations@hoteldavid.it
To: mary.tan@infotec.ch
Date: 3 August 20– –
Subject: change of dates

Dear Ms Tan
Regarding your email requesting a change of dates, we confirm your new booking of 1 double and 1 single room for 2 nights from 9 to 11 June.

We have reserved a parking space for you from the evening of 9 June to the morning of 11 June as requested.

We also confirm your restaurant reservation for a table for 3 at 8.30 p.m. on 9 June.

We look forward to welcoming you to Hotel David.
Best regards

Reservations
Hotel David

Letter

Mr Piet van Derbilt
Amstel 140
1017 EZ Amsterdam

Crowne Plaza Hotel
rue de la Roi 107
1040 Brussels
21 March 20– –

Dear Mr van Derbilt
Thank you very much for your recent enquiry regarding organizing a business lunch for 60 people at the Crowne Plaza Hotel on Friday 30th May.

We are delighted to be able to offer you our charming Grapevine Restaurant on that afternoon. The restaurant will be available for you and your guests from 12 noon until 3 p.m. We enclose sample menus for you to choose from.

The Crowne Plaza is in the city centre, five minutes' walk from the railway station. I enclose a map for your information.

Unfortunately, we do not have on-site parking at the hotel but there is a large public car park, which is only a three-minute walk from the hotel.

We look forward very much to hearing from you.
Yours sincerely

(signature)

(word processed name)
Events Manager

Curriculum vitae

Name ....

Address ....
....

Home telephone ....
Mobile ....
Email ....

Profile
(example)

I am a highly-motivated and hard-working person. I can work equally well as a team member or using my own initiative.
I think my skills and experience would be a valuable addition to your department. I would be an enthusiastic team member and enjoy the challenges of pursuing my career and using my skills in another country.

Education ....
....

Qualifications ....
....
....

Career history/
Work experience ....
....
....

Responsibilities/
Achievements ....
....

Interests ....

References ....
....

Interview assessment sheet

Student's name
....

Job applied for
....

	Ratings
Punctuality	☐
Appearance	☐
Manner	☐
Attitude	☐
Motivation	☐
Suitability	☐
Confidence	☐
Level of interest shown	☐
Relevant experience	☐
Answering questions	☐
Body language	☐
Evidence of preparation for interview	☐
Asking questions	☐
Overall impression	☐

Rating: 1 – good/appropriate
2 – average/acceptable
3 – below average/needs further work
x – unable to make an assessment

OXFORD
UNIVERSITY PRESS

Great Clarendon Street, Oxford OX2 6DP

Oxford University Press is a department of the University of Oxford.
It furthers the University's objective of excellence in research, scholarship,
and education by publishing worldwide in

Oxford New York

Auckland Cape Town Dar es Salaam Hong Kong Karachi
Kuala Lumpur Madrid Melbourne Mexico City Nairobi
New Delhi Shanghai Taipei Toronto

With offices in

Argentina Austria Brazil Chile Czech Republic France Greece
Guatemala Hungary Italy Japan Poland Portugal Singapore
South Korea Switzerland Thailand Turkey Ukraine Vietnam

OXFORD and OXFORD ENGLISH are registered trade marks of
Oxford University Press in the UK and in certain other countries

ISBN: 978 0 19 457752 6

Printed in China

This book is printed on paper from certified and well-managed sources.

ACKNOWLEDGEMENTS

*The author and publisher would like to thank the following people who assisted in
the development of this Teacher's Book*: Roger Nicholson - L'Escola Universitària
de Turisme i Direcció Hotelera de la Universitat Autònoma de Barcelona
(EUTDH - UAB), Barcelona, Spain, for the idea of the 'One-upmanship' game, p.9.

Cover image courtesy: Alamy Images (chef/Tetra Images)

*Although every effort has been made to trace and contact copyright holders before
publication, this has not been possible in some cases. We apologize for any apparent
infringement of copyright and if notified, the publisher will be pleased to rectify any
errors or omissions at the earliest opportunity.*

*Oxford University Press makes no representation, express or implied, that the advice
or procedures described in this book are correct. Readers must therefore always check
procedures with the most up-to-date information in their country and the most recent
codes of conduct and safety regulations.*

*The authors and the publishers do not accept responsibility or legal liability for any
errors in the text or for the misuse or misapplication of material in this work.*